The Economics
of Contracts

The Economics of Contracts

A Primer

Bernard Salanié

The MIT Press
Cambridge, Massachusetts
London, England

Third printing, 1999

English translation © 1997 Massachusetts Institute of Technology. Originally published in French under the title *Théorie des contracts.* © 1994 Economica, Paris.

This book was set in Palatino by Omegatype, Inc.

Printed and bound in the United States of America.

Library of Congress Cataloging-in-Publication Data

Salanié, Bernard.
  [Theorie des contrats. English]
  The economics of contracts : primer / Bernard Salanié.
     p.   cm.
  Includes bibliographical references and index.
  IBSN 0-262-19386-8 (alk. paper)
  1. Contracts—Economic aspects. I. Title.
K840.S25   1997
346'.02—dc20
[342.62]   96-44901
                                                  CIP

Contents

Foreword

This book aims at introducing Ph.D. students and professional economists to the theory of contracts. It originated in graduate-level courses I gave at Stanford University and at ENSAE (Ecole Nationale de la Statistique et de l'Administration Economique) to third-year students. This book has benefited from discussions with these students.

The course notes were published as *Théorie des contrats* in France by Economica. The present book is a fully revised, somewhat expanded, and hopefully improved translation of that book.

I am grateful to Jérôme Accardo, Jérôme Philippe, Patrick Rey, and two anonymous reviewers, who read a first draft of the French version and provided very useful comments. I also thank Bruno Jullien, Jean-Jacques Laffont, Tom Palfrey, François Salanié, Jean Tirole, and three anonymous reviewers who read all or part of the English version and greatly helped me improve it. My intellectual debt extends to my coauthors in this field, Pierre-André Chiappori and Patrick Rey, and to Guy Laroque, who was a very effective and critical tutor when I started doing research in economics.

Finally, I thank Terry Vaughn and the MIT Press for their encouragement and support in this project. Needless to say, I am solely responsible for any errors or imperfections that may remain in the book.

The Economics
of Contracts

1   Introduction

The theory of general equilibrium is one of the most impressive achievements in the history of economic thought. In the 1950s and 1960s the proof of the existence of equilibrium and of the close correspondence among equilibria, Pareto optima, and the core seemed to open the way for a reconstruction of the whole of economic theory around these concepts. However, it appeared rapidly that the general equilibrium model was not a fully satisfactory descriptive tool. Strategic interactions between agents indeed are heavily constrained in that model: Agents only interact through the price system, which the pure competition assumption says they cannot influence. In the logical limit one gets the models of the Aumann-Hildenbrand school in which there is a continuum of nonatomic agents, none of whom can influence equilibrium prices and allocations. Similarly the organization of the many institutions that govern economic relationships is totally absent from these models. This is particularly striking in the case of firms, which are modeled as a production set. Indeed, the very existence of firms is difficult to justify in the context of general equilibrium models, since all interactions take place through the price system in these models. As Coase said long ago in one of his most influential papers (Coase 1937), "The distinguishing mark of the firm is the supersession of the price mechanism."

Taking into account informational asymmetries is another challenge for general equilibrium models. As Arrow and Debreu showed, it is fairly straightforward to extend the general equilibrium model to cover uncertainty as long as information stays symmetric. Unfortunately, asymmetries of information are pervasive in economic relationships: Customers know more about their tastes than firms, firms know more about their costs than the government, and all agents take actions that are at least partly unobservable. Rational expectations equilibria were conceived at least in part to encompass asymmetric information. However, while they offer interesting insights on the revelation of information by prices, their treatment of asymmetric information is not quite satisfactory. A *homo œconomicus* who possesses private information should be expected to try to manipulate it, since he has in effect a monopoly over his own piece of private information. If we want to take this into account, we need to resort to other tools and, in particular, to game theory.

The theory of contracts originates in these failures of general equilibrium theory. In the 1970s, several economists settled on a new way to study economic relationships. The idea was to turn away temporarily from general equilibrium models, whose description of the economy is consistent but not realistic enough, and to focus on necessarily partial models that take into account the full complexity of strategic interactions between privately informed agents in well-defined institutional settings. It was hoped then that lessons drawn from these studies could later be integrated inside a better theory of general equilibrium.

The theory of contracts, and more generally what was called the "economics of information," were the tools used to explore this new domain. Because they are just that—tools—it is somewhat difficult to define their goals other than by contrasting their shared characteristics with previous approaches:

· For the most part, they are partial equilibrium models; they isolate the markets for one good (sometimes two goods) from the rest of the economy.

• They describe the interactions of a small number of agents (often just two, one of whom possesses some private information and is call the "informed party").

• They sum up the constraints imposed by the prevailing institutional setting through a *contract*. This may be explicit and embodied in a written agreement. It may also be implicit if it relies on a system of behavioral norms, for instance. An explicit contract will be guaranteed by a "third party" (e.g., a court or a mediator) or by the desire agents have to maintain a reputation for fair trading. An implicit contract will need to be sustained as an equilibrium in the interaction between the parties.

• These models make an intensive use of noncooperative game theory with asymmetric information, although their description of the bargaining process generally relies on the simplistic device known as the principal-agent model (on which more later in this introduction). They are embedded in a Bayesian universe in which parties have an a priori belief on the information they do not possess, and they revise this belief as the interaction unfolds. The equilibrium concept they use indeed belongs to the family of perfect Bayesian equilibria.

The theory of contracts obviously covers a lot of ground and many varied situations. As a consequence early empirical studies were mostly case studies. Only recently has a body of literature emerged that tries to test the main conclusions of the theory of contracts using standard structural econometric techniques.

1.1   The Great Families of Models

The models of the theory of contracts can be distinguished along several axes, whether they be static or dynamic, whether they involve complete or incomplete contracts, whether they describe a bilateral or multilateral relationship, and so on. There is a large class of models which can easily be divided into three families: those where an informed party meets an uninformed party. I have chosen, somewhat arbitrarily of course, to classify these models according to two criteria: first, whether the private information bears on

• what the agent *does*, the decisions he takes ("hidden action"),

• who the agent *is*, what his characteristics are ("hidden information");

Second, according to the form of the strategic game. I will distinguish models in which the initiative belongs to the uninformed party from those in which it belongs to the informed party.

This classification yields three important families[1]:

• In *adverse selection* models, the uninformed party is imperfectly informed of the characteristics of the informed party; the uninformed party moves first.

• In *signaling* models, the informational situation is the same but the informed party moves first.

• In *moral hazard* models, the uninformed party moves first and is imperfectly informed of the actions of the informed party.

Chapters 2 to 5 will study the basic models in each of these three families. I should mention here, however, that one important class of models does not fit this classification: models of incomplete contracting, which have so far only been developed in situations of symmetric information. They are studied in chapter 7.

1.2   The Principal-Agent Model

Most of this book will use the Principal-Agent paradigm. There are two economic agents in this model: the informed party, whose information is relevant for the common welfare, and the uninformed

---

1. The fourth case is that where the uninformed party does not observe the actions of the informed party and the latter takes the initiative of the contract. It is difficult to imagine a real-world application of such a model; in any case I do not know of any paper that uses it.

party. Since this is a bilateral monopoly situation, we cannot go very far unless we specify how the parties are going to bargain over the terms of exchange. Unfortunately, the study of bargaining under asymmetric information is very complex, so much so that there is presently no consensus among theorists on what equilibrium concept should be used.[2] The Principal-Agent model is a simplifying device that avoids these difficulties by allocating all bargaining power to one of the parties. This party will propose a "take it or leave it" contract and therefore request a "yes or no" answer; the other party is not free to propose another contract.

The Principal-Agent game is therefore a Stackelberg game in which the *leader* (who proposes the contract) is called the Principal and the *follower* (the party who just has to accept or reject the contract) is called the Agent.[3] While this modeling choice makes things much simpler, the reader should keep in mind that actual bargaining procedures are likely to be much more complex. For instance, if the Agent indeed rejects the contract, the interaction stops in the Principal-Agent model, whereas in the real world it should be expected to continue.

Since the book relies so heavily upon the Principal-Agent model, let me discuss it a bit. One way to justify the Principal-Agent paradigm is to observe that the set of (constrained) Pareto optima can always be obtained by maximizing the utility of one agent while the other is held to a given utility level. This is precisely what the Principal-Agent model does; so if we are only interested in common properties of the optima and not in one particular optimum, this approach brings no loss of generality. On the other hand, it may be that reasons outside the model should make us fix the Agent's reservation utility at some given level; if, for instance, the Principal is an employer and the

2. The main difficulty is that the natural equilibrium concept, sequential equilibrium, leads to a large multiplicity of equilibria. See Binmore-Osborne-Rubinstein (1992) for a recent survey of bargaining models.
3. I have tried to use consistent notation throughout the book: thus the "Agent" will always be the follower in a Principal-Agent game, while an "agent" is simply an economic agent, so that the Principal is also an agent. I hope this will cause no confusion.

Agent a prospective employee, the level of unemployment benefits and/or the market wage determine his reservation utility. In that case the peculiar properties of the Principal-Agent bargaining solution— it gives all surplus to the Principal—may make it less attractive as it picks a single point on the utility possibility frontier. Finally, let me mention an apparent paradox. We will see later that in adverse selection models the Principal generally leaves zero utility to at least one type of Agent. But what if the Agent must incur a cost to participate in the relationship (e.g., if he must take a train to the place of an auction)? In that case Salanié (1996) shows that no type of Agent will ever want to participate.[4] Of course the paradox can be solved by assuming that the Principal can commit ex ante to leave a given surplus to the Agent provided that such a commitment is realistic. Still it shows that the Principal-Agent model is a rather extreme and therefore fragile modeling assumption.

Finally, the choice of the words "Principal" and "Agent" should not be taken to imply that one of the parties works for the other or that the modeler is more interested in one than in the other. Each model has its own logic and should be interpreted accordingly. I should also point out that this terminology is taken by several authors, starting with the pioneering paper by Ross (1973), to refer to what they call the problem of agency, which is a moral hazard problem. My use of the Principal-Agent paradigm is both wider and more abstract; to me, it basically means that a Stackelberg game is being played.

1.3 Overview of the Book

An exhaustive book on the theory of contracts and its applications would be very thick indeed. Such is not my ambition here. I merely want to present the main models of the theory of contracts, and par-

---

4. Similar results can be found in the literature on bargaining with incomplete information.

ticularly the basic models of the three great families described in section 1.1. It is not always easy to determine what belongs to the theory of contracts and what belongs to the wider field of the economics of information. I have chosen to include a brief description of auction models because their study relies on the same tools as the theory of contracts. On the other hand, I have preferred not to give a central role to models of insurance markets, even though their historical importance in shaping the field is well-established. As I will argue in section 3.1.3, these models have some peculiar features, and they deserve a fuller treatment than I can give them in such a short book.

I have deliberately chosen to emphasize the methods used to analyze the models of the theory of contracts rather than the many applications that it has generated in various fields of economics. I have included brief introductions to these applications, but without any claim to completeness; most of these applications are not solved out in the text. The reader will have to decide for himself what application he is interested in; I urge him to peruse the lists of references and to read the original papers. My goal in writing this book was to give the basic tools that will allow the reader to understand the basic models and to create his own. I have tried to include recent developments, except where this led to overtechnical analyses. In most cases the lists of references should be sufficiently rich to allow the reader to find his way through this burgeoning literature.

Chapter 2 presents the general theory of adverse selection models. It starts with a brief summary of mechanism design, then solves a basic model of second-degree price discrimination with two types; it then presents the solution in a more general continuous-type model. Several examples of applications and some more recent extensions are studied in chapter 3.

Chapter 4 studies signaling models, both when signals are costly and when they are free.

I study the basic moral hazard model, some of its extensions and its application to insurance and wage contracts in chapter 5.

Chapter 6 is dedicated to the dynamic aspects of the theory of complete contracts: commitment, renegotiation, . . . that have been at the forefront of recent research. Because that field is very technical, I have not tried to prove most results in that chapter. This is a clear case where interested readers should refer to the original papers.

Chapter 7 introduces the theory of incomplete contracts, which has developed in the last ten years or so and is still at an immature stage.

Finally, chapter 8 concludes the book by examining the empirical and econometric literature based on the theory of contracts. The emphasis in that chapter is on structural models.

This is a fairly formal book, judging by the number of equations. However, mathematical requirements for reading this book are low: Elementary notions of calculus should be sufficient. The only exceptions occur in chapters 4 and 6, which use somewhat more advanced notions of noncooperative game theory. An appendix presents these concepts for the readers who might need them. I have also starred a couple of sections that are more involved and can be skipped if necessary.

My original plan did not call for exercises; however, I found when writing the book that several came to mind. Thus chapters 2 to 5 end with a list of exercises.

References

Works Cited

Binmore, K., M. Osborne, and A. Rubinstein. 1992. Non-cooperative models of bargaining. In *Handbook of Game Theory*, vol. 1, R. Aumann and S. Hart, eds. North-Holland.

Coase, R. 1937. The nature of the firm. *Economica* 4:386–405.

Ross, S. 1973. The economic theory of agency: The principal's problem. *American Economic Review* 63:134–39.

Salanié, F. 1996. A difficulty with the principal-agent model. Mimeo. INRA-Toulouse.

General References

I know of only one other textbook that takes the theory of contracts as its subject:

Macho-Stadler, I., and D. Perez-Castrillo, 1997. *An Introduction to the Economics of Information: Incentives and Contracts.* Oxford: Oxford University Press.

However, several books dedicate some space to the theory. Their approaches should be viewed as complementary to mine.

Diamond, P., and M. Rothschild. 1989. *Uncertainty in Economics.* San Diego: Academic Press.
A book of readings that collects and puts into perspective many important papers.

Fudenberg, D., and J. Tirole. 1991. *Game Theory.* Cambridge: MIT Press.
A rather formal textbook that contains results relevant to the theory of contracts, especially in chapter 7.

Hirshleifer, J., and J. Riley. 1992. *The Analytics of Uncertainty and Information.* Cambridge: Cambridge University Press.
Useful for chapters 8 and 11.

Kreps, D. 1990. *A Course in Microeconomic Theory.* Princeton: Princeton University Press.
A very accessible text; readers of this book should mainly be concerned with chapters 16 to 18.

Laffont, J.-J. 1989. *The Economics of Uncertainty and Information.* Cambridge: MIT Press.
A book that is more analytical and much more concise than Kreps's; see chapters 8, 10, and 11 and also the problems at the end of the book.

Laffont, J.-J., and J. Tirole. 1993. *A Theory of Incentives in Procurement and Regulation.* Cambridge: MIT Press.
A very complete book on procurement and the regulation of firms that contains many chapters of more general interest, especially on the dynamics of complete contracts.

Mas-Colell, A., M. Whinston, and J. Green. 1995. *Microeconomic Theory.* Oxford: Oxford University Press.
An excellent graduate textbook that devotes its chapters 13 and 14 to theory of contracts models.

Milgrom, P., and J. Roberts. 1992. *Economics, Organization and Management.* Englewood Cliffs, NJ: Prentice Hall.
Not really a theory book, but it presents in detail several key applications of the theory of contracts in the context of firms; it is highly readable.

Rasmusen, E. 1989. *Games and Information*. Oxford: Basil Blackwell.
A game-theoretic study of theory of contracts models can be found in part II of this book.

Tirole, J. 1988. *Industrial Organization*. Cambridge: MIT Press.
For many examples of applications of the theory of contracts and also for chapter 11, the best introduction I know to perfect Bayesian equilibria.

2 Adverse Selection: General Theory

We use the term "adverse selection" when a characteristic of the Agent is imperfectly observed by the Principal.[1] This term comes from a phenomenon well-known to insurers: If a company only offers a tariff tailored to the average risk in the population, this tariff will only attract the higher risks and will therefore lose money. This effect may even induce the insurer to give up insuring some risks. Other terms sometimes used are "self-selection" and "screening." The general idea of adverse selection can be grasped on the following example, which I will analyze in detail in section 2.2.

Let the Principal be a wine seller and the Agent a buyer. The Agent may be a keen amateur of good wines or he may have more modest tastes. We will say there are two "types": the sophisticated Agent (who is ready to pay a large sum for a great vintage) and the coarse Agent (whose tastes—or means—are less developed).

I will assume that the Principal cannot observe the type of any given Agent, or at least that the law (as is often the case) forbids him to use nonanonymous prices that would discriminate between the two types.[2]

The key to the solution of the adverse selection problem is the following observation: If the sophisticated Agent is willing to pay more

---

1. Recall that this chapter and the following use the Principal-Agent paradigm introduced in section 1.2.
2. Thus in Pigou's terms, first-degree price discrimination is unfeasible or at least illegal.

than the coarse Agent for a given increase in the quality of the wine, then the Principal can segment the market by offering two different wine bottles:

$$\begin{cases} \text{a wine of high quality for a high price} \\ \text{a wine of lower quality for a lower price} \end{cases}$$

We will see in section 2.2 how these qualities and prices are to be chosen optimally.

If all goes according to plan, the sophisticated type will choose the high-quality–high-price wine, while the coarse one will pick the lower-quality bottle. Thus the two types of Agent "reveal themselves" through their choice of a wine. As we will see, this implies that the coarse type buys a lower quality than would be socially optimal. The whole point of adverse selection problems is to make the Agents reveal their type without incurring too high a social distortion.

Let me briefly quote a few other examples:

• In the context of life insurance, the insured know their own state of health (and therefore their risk of dying soon) better than does the insurer, even if they have to go through a medical visit. This suggest that the insurer should offer several insurance packages, each tailored for a specific risk class. I will study this situation in section 3.1.3.

• Banks customarily face borrowers whose default risk they can only imperfectly assess: for instance, entrepreneurs who want financing for risky projects. A natural idea is to use interest rates to discriminate between entrepreneurs. However, this may induce credit rationing, unless banks also vary collateral levels.[3]

• On labor markets, employers face potential workers who have an informational advantage in that they know their innate abilities better than firms. The latter then must screen the workers so as to attract the gifted and discard the others.

---

3. This is an admittedly very skimpy summary of a body of literature that started with Stiglitz-Weiss (1981).

· Many firms (state-owned or not) are regulated by the government or by a specialized agency. Clearly the regulated firm has more information on its costs or its productivity than the regulator. This implies that it will try to manipulate the way it discloses information to the regulator so as to increase its profits (see section 3.1.1).

*2.1   Mechanism Design

The theory of mechanism design is the basis for the study of adverse selection models, so much so that some authors also call adverse selection models "mechanism design problems." I will not attempt here to give a self-contained presentation of mechanism design. I will assume that the reader has already been exposed to this theory, and my sole aim will be to remind him of the general formalism and of the results that I will need later.[4] This section may seem abstract to some readers; they can skip it without losing the thread of the chapter.

The object of the theory of mechanism design is to explore the means of implementing a given allocation of available resources when the relevant information is dispersed in the economy. Take, for instance, a social choice problem in which each agent $i = 1, ..., n$ has some relevant private information θ_i, and assume that despite all the reservations exemplified by Arrow's theorem, society has decided that the optimal allocation is

$$y(\theta) = (y_1(\theta_1, ..., \theta_n), ..., y_n(\theta_1, ..., \theta_n))$$

This would (presumably) be easy to implement if the government knew all the θ_i's. However, if only i knows his θ_i and, say, his optimal allocation $y_i(\theta)$ increases with θ_i, he is very likely to overstate his θ_i so as to obtain a larger allocation. This can make it very difficult to implement $y(\theta)$.

The provision of public goods is another example. Everybody benefits from a bridge, but nobody particularly cares to contribute to

---

4. See Laffont (1989) or Moore (1992) for a more complete exposition.

its building costs. The optimal financing scheme would presumably depend on each agent's potential use for the bridge: for example, heavy commuters would pay more than sedentary types. In the absence of a reliable way to differentiate individuals, the government will have to rely on voluntary declarations where, naturally, every agent understates the utility he derives from the bridge. This may even cause the bridge not to be built, since its cost may exceed its reported benefits.

As a final example, consider the implementation of a Walrasian equilibrium in an exchange economy. We all know that this has very good properties under the usual assumptions. However, it is not clear how the economy can move to a Walrasian equilibrium. If information were publicly available, the government could just compute the equilibrium and give all consumers their equilibrium allocations.[5] In practice, the agents' utility functions (or their true demand functions) are their private information, and they can be expected to lie so as to maximize their utility. As information is dispersed throughout the economy, implementable allocations are subject to a large number of incentive constraints.

In all of these examples, two related questions arise:

• Can $y(\theta)$ be implemented? In other words, is it incentive compatible (some authors say "feasible")?

• What is the optimal choice among incentive compatible allocations?

In more abstract terms, we consider a situation in which

• there are n agents $i = 1, \ldots, n$ characterized by parameters $\theta_i \in \Theta_i$ which are their private information and are often called their "types";

• agents are facing a "Center" who wants to implement a given allocation of resources, and generally (which is of course the interesting case) this allocation will depend on the agents' private characteristics θ_i.

---

5. This was the original vision of the proponents of market socialism.

I will not be precise as to what the Center represents. Think of it as the government, or as some economic agent who has been given the responsibility for implementing an allocation, or even as an abstraction such as the Walras auctioneer. The Center needn't be a benevolent dictator; he may be, for instance, the seller of a good who wants to extract as much surplus as possible from agents whose valuations for the good he cannot observe.

2.1.1 General Mechanisms

The problem facing the Center is an incentive problem: He must try to extract information from the agents so that he can implement the right allocation. To do this, the Center may resort to very complicated procedures, using bribes to urge the agents to reveal some of their private information. This process, however complicated, can be summed up in a *mechanism* $(y(.), M_1, \ldots, M_n)$. This consists of a message space M_i for each agent i and a function $y(.)$ from $M_1 \times \ldots \times M_n$ to the set of feasible allocations. The allocation rule $y(.) = (y_1(.), \ldots, y_n(.))$ determines the allocations of all n agents as a function of the messages they send to the Center.[6] Note that these allocations generally are vectors.

Given an allocation rule $y(.)$, the agents play a message game in which the message spaces M_i are their strategy sets and the allocation rule $y(.)$ determines their allocations and therefore their utility levels. Agent i then chooses a message m_i in M and sends it to the Center, who imposes the allocation $y(m_1, \ldots, m_n)$.

Note that in general, the message chosen by agent i will depend on his information I_i, which contains his characteristic θ_i but may in fact be richer, as will be the case, for instance, if each agent knows that characteristic of members of his family or perhaps of his neighbors. Equilibrium messages thus will be functions $m_i^*(I_i)$ and the implemented allocation will be

---

6. The most general mechanism would allow for stochastic allocation rules. Here I will assume that they are deterministic.

$$y^*(I_1, \ldots, I_n) = y\big(m_1^*(I_1), \ldots, m_n^*(I_n)\big)$$

Assume that the Center is the proverbial Walrasian auctioneer and tries to implement a Walrasian equilibrium in a context in which he does not know the agents' preferences. Then one way for him to proceed is to ask the agents for their demand functions, to compute the corresponding equilibrium, and to give each agent his equilibrium allocation. If he were the builder of a bridge, he might announce a rule stating on which conditions he will decide to build the bridge and how it will be financed; then he would ask each agent for his willingness to pay.

2.1.2 Application to Adverse Selection Models

The models we are concerned with in this chapter are a very special and simple instance of mechanism design. The Principal here is the Center, while the Agent is the only agent. Thus $n = 1$, and the information I of the Agent boils down to his type θ. Given a mechanism $(y(.), M)$, the Agent chooses the message he sends so as to maximize his utility $u(y, \theta)$:

$$m^*(\theta) \in \arg \max_{m \in M} u(y(m), \theta)$$

and he obtains the corresponding allocation

$$y^*(\theta) = y(m^*(\theta))$$

The revelation principle below[7] implies that one can confine attention to mechanisms that are both *direct* (where the Agent reports his information) and *truthful* (so that the Agent finds it optimal to announce the true value of his information).

---

7. I only state this principle for the case when $n = 1$; it is valid in a much more general case, but the shape it takes depends on the equilibrium concept one uses for the message-sending game between the n agents. These complications needn't concern us here.

Revelation Principle

If the allocation $y^*(\theta)$ can be implemented through some mechanism, then it can also be implemented through a direct truthful mechanism where the Agent reveals his information θ.

The proof of this result is elementary. Let $(y(.), M)$ be a mechanism that implements the allocation y^*, and let $m^*(\theta)$ be the equilibrium message, so that $y^* = y \circ m^*$. Now consider the direct mechanism $(y^*(.), \Theta)$. If it were not truthful, then an Agent would prefer to announce some θ' rather than his true type θ, and we would have

$$u(y^*(\theta), \theta) < u(y^*(\theta'), \theta)$$

But by the definition of y^*, this would imply that

$$u(y(m^*(\theta)), \theta) < u(y(m^*(\theta')), \theta)$$

so that m^* would not be an equilibrium in the game generated by the mechanism $(y(.), M)$, since the Agent of type θ would prefer to announce $m^*(\theta')$ rather than $m^*(\theta)$. Thus the direct mechanism (y^*, Θ) must be truthful, and by construction, it implements the allocation y^*.

Note that in a direct mechanism the message space of the Agent coincides with his type space. Thus in the example of the bridge, the Agent needs only to announce his willingness to pay.

Assume that, as is often the case, the allocation y consists of an allocation q and a monetary transfer p. The revelation principle states that to implement the quantity allocation $q(\theta)$ using transfers $p(\theta)$, it is enough to offer the Agent a menu of contracts: If the Agent announces that his type is θ, he will receive the allocation $q(\theta)$ and will pay the transfer $p(\theta)$.

Direct truthful mechanisms are very simple. However, they rely on messages that do not seem very realistic a priori; in the example of the wine seller, it is difficult to imagine the buyer coming into the shop and declaring "I am sophisticated" or "I am coarse." A second result sometimes called the *taxation principle* comes to our help by showing that these mechanisms are equivalent to a nonlinear tariff $\tau(.)$ that lets the Agent choose an allocation q and makes him pay a corresponding transfer $p = \tau(q)$. The proof of this principle again is very simple. Let there be two types θ and θ' such that $q(\theta) = q(\theta')$; if $p(\theta)$ were larger than $p(\theta')$, then the Agent of type θ would pretend to be of type θ', and the mechanism could not be truthful. Therefore we must have $p(\theta) = p(\theta')$, and the function $\tau(.)$ can be defined unambiguously by

if $q = q(\theta)$,   then $\tau(q) = p(\theta)$

In our earlier example the wine seller just needs to offer the buyer two wine bottles that are differentiated by their quality and price. This is of course much more realistic; even though most retailers do not post a nonlinear tariff on their doors, they often use a system of rebates that approximates a nonlinear tariff.

2.2   A Discrete Model of Price Discrimination

In section 2.3, I will give the general solution of the standard adverse selection model with a continuous set of types. Here I want first to derive the optimum in a simple two-type model, relying heavily on graphical techniques and very simple arguments.

To simplify things, I will reuse my example of a wine seller who offers wines of different qualities (and different prices) in order to segment a market in which consumers' tastes differ. This is therefore a model that exhibits both vertical differentiation and second-degree price discrimination.[8]

2.2.1   The Consumer

Let the Agent be a moderate drinker who plans to buy at most one bottle of wine within the period we study. His utility is $U = \theta q - t$,

---

8. The classic reference for this model is Mussa-Rosen (1978), who use a continuous set of types.

where q is the quality he buys and θ is a positive parameter that indexes his taste for quality. If he decides not to buy any wine, his utility is just 0.

Note that with this specification,

$$\forall \theta' > \theta, \quad u(q, \theta') - u(q, \theta) \quad \text{increases in } q$$

This is the discrete form of what I will call the Spence-Mirrlees condition in section 2.3. For now, just note its economic significance: At any given quality level, the more sophisticated consumers are willing to pay more than the coarse consumers for the same increase in quality. This is what gives us the hope that we will be able to segment the market on quality.

There are two possible values for θ: $\theta_1 < \theta_2$; the prior probability that the Agent is of type 1 (or the proportion of types 1 in the population) is π. In the following, I will call "sophisticated" the consumers of type 2 and "coarse" the consumers of type 1.

2.2.2   The Seller

The Principal is a local monopoly on the wine market. He can produce wine of any quality $q \in (0, \infty)$; the production of a bottle of quality q costs him $C(q)$. I will assume that C is twice differentiable and strictly convex, that $C'(0) = 0$ and $C'(\infty) = \infty$.

The utility of the Principal is just the difference between his receipts and his costs, or $t - C(q)$.

2.2.3   The First-Best: Perfect Discrimination

If the producer can observe the type θ_i of the consumer, he will solve the following program:

$$\max_{q_i, t_i} (t_i - C(q_i))$$

$$\theta_i q_i - t_i \geq 0$$

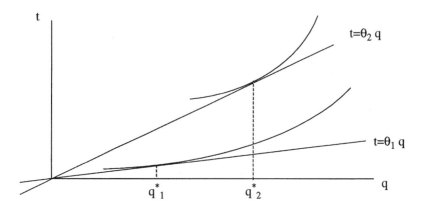

Figure 2.1
The first-best contracts

He will therefore offer $q_i = q_i^*$ such that $C'(q_i^*) = \theta_i$ and $t_i^* = \theta_i q_i^*$ to the consumer of type θ_i, thus extracting all his surplus; the consumer will be left with zero utility.

Figure 2.1 represents the two first-best contracts in the plane (q, t). The two lines shown are the indifference lines corresponding to zero utility for the two types of Agent. The curves tangent to them are iso-profit curves, with equation $t = C(q) + K$. Their convexity is a consequence of our assumptions on the function C. Note that the utility of the Agent increases when going southeast, while the profit of the Principal increases when going northwest.

q_1^* and q_2^* are the "efficient qualities." Since $\theta_1 < \theta_2$ and C' is increasing, we get $q_2^* > q_1^*$, and the sophisticated consumer buys a higher quality wine than the coarse consumer.

This type of discrimination, called first-degree price discrimination, is generally forbidden by the law, according to which the sale should be anonymous: You cannot refuse a consumer a deal you accepted for another consumer.[9] However, we are now going to study the case where the seller cannot observe directly the con-

---

9. As we will see shortly, the sophisticated consumer envies the coarse consumer's deal.

sumer's type; then perfect discrimination becomes unfeasible, whatever its legal status.

2.2.4   Imperfect Information

Let us now turn to the second-best situation in which information is asymmetric. The producer now only knows that the proportion of coarse consumers is π. If he proposes the first-best contracts (q_1^*, t_1^*), (q_2^*, t_2^*), the sophisticated consumers will not choose (q_2^*, t_2^*) but (q_1^*, t_1^*), since

$$\theta_2 q_1^* - t_1^* = (\theta_2 - \theta_1) q_1^* > 0 = \theta_2 q_2^* - t_2^*$$

The two types are not separated any more: Both will choose the low-quality deal (q_1^*, t_1^*).

Nevertheless, the producer can get higher profits by proposing, for instance, (q_1^*, t_1^*) and the point designated by A in figure 2.2; A will then be chosen by the sophisticates and only by them. Note that A is located on a higher isoprofit curve than (q_1^*, t_1^*), and therefore it gives a higher profit to the seller.

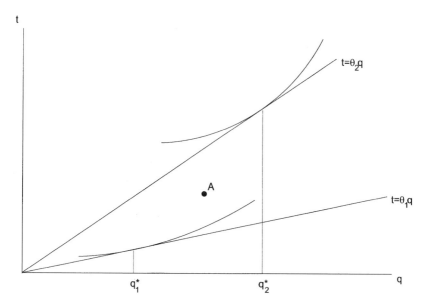

Figure 2.2
A potentially improving contract

Many other contracts are even better than A. Our concern is with the best pair of contracts (the second-best optimum), which is obtained by solving the following program:

$$\max_{t_1, q_1, t_2, q_2} \{\pi[t_1 - C(q_1)] + (1 - \pi)[t_2 - C(q_2)]\}$$

subject to

$$\begin{cases} \theta_1 q_1 - t_1 \geq \theta_1 q_2 - t_2 & (IC_1) \\ \theta_2 q_2 - t_2 \geq \theta_2 q_1 - t_1 & (IC_2) \\ \theta_1 q_1 - t_1 \geq 0 & (IR_1) \\ \theta_2 q_2 - t_2 \geq 0 & (IR_2) \end{cases}$$

Note the names of the constraints in this program:

• The two (IC) constraints are the *incentive compatibility* constraints; they state that each consumer prefers the contract that was designed for him

• The two (IR) constraints are the *individual rationality*, or *participation* constraints; they guarantee that each type of consumer accepts his designated contract.

We will prove that at the optimum:

1. (IR_1) is active, so $t_1 = \theta_1 q_1$

2. (IC_2) is active, whence

$$t_2 - t_1 = \theta_2(q_2 - q_1)$$

3. $q_2 \geq q_1$.

4. We can neglect (IC_1) and (IR_2).

5. Sophisticated consumers buy the efficient quality:

$$q_2 = q_2^*$$

Proofs   We use (IC_2) to prove property 1.

$$\theta_2 q_2 - t_2 \geq \theta_2 q_1 - t_1 \geq \theta_1 q_1 - t_1$$

since $q_1 \geq 0$ and $\theta_2 > \theta_1$. If (IR_1) was inactive, so would be (IR_2), and we could increase t_1 and t_2 by the same amount. This would increase the Principal's profit without any effect on incentive compatibility.

Property 2 is proved by assuming that (IC_2) is inactive. Then

$$\theta_2 q_2 - t_2 > \theta_2 q_1 - t_1 \geq \theta_1 q_1 - t_1 = 0$$

We can therefore augment t_2 without breaking incentive compatibility or the individual rationality constraint (IR_2). This obviously increases the Principal's profit, and therefore the original mechanism cannot be optimal.

To prove property 3, let us add (IC_1) and (IC_2). The transfers t_i cancel out, and we get

$$\theta_2(q_2 - q_1) \geq \theta_1(q_2 - q_1)$$

and $q_2 - q_1 \geq 0$, since $\theta_2 > \theta_1$.

For property 4, (IC_1) can be neglected since (IC_2) is active, so using property 3,

$$t_2 - t_1 = \theta_2(q_2 - q_1) \geq \theta_1(q_2 - q_1)$$

The proof of assertion 1 shows that (IR_2) can be neglected.

Finally, for property 5, let us prove that $C'(q_2) = \theta_2$. If $C'(q_2) < \theta_2$, for instance, let ε be a small positive number, and consider the new mechanism (q_1, t_1), $(q_2' = q_2 + \varepsilon, t_2' = t_2 + \varepsilon\theta_2)$. It is easily seen that

$$\theta_2 q_2' - t_2' = \theta_2 q_2 - t_2 \text{ and } \theta_1 q_2' - t_2' = \theta_1 q_2 - t_2 - \varepsilon(\theta_2 - \theta_1)$$

so that the new mechanism satisfies all four constraints. Moreover

$$t_2' - C(q_2') \simeq t_2 - C(q_2) + \varepsilon(\theta_2 - C'(q_2))$$

and the new mechanism yields higher profits than the original one, which is absurd. We can prove in the same way that $C'(q_2) > \theta_2$ is impossible (just change the sign of ε).

It is an easy and useful exercise to obtain graphical proofs of these five points.

The optimal pair of contracts thus appears to be located as on figure 2.3: (q_1, t_1) is on the zero utility indifference line of the Agent of type 1 and (q_2, t_2) is the tangency point between an isoprofit curve of the seller and the indifference line of the Agent of type 2 that goes through (q_2, t_2).

To fully characterize the optimal pair of contracts, we just have to let (q_1, t_1) in figure 2.3 slide on the line $t_1 = \theta_1 q_1$. Formally the optimum is obtained by replacing q_2 with q_2^* and expressing the values of t_1 and t_2 as functions of q_1, using

$$\begin{cases} t_1 = \theta_1 q_1 \\ t_2 - t_1 = \theta_2(q_2 - q_1) \end{cases}$$

This gives

$$\begin{cases} q_2 = q_2^* \\ t_1 = \theta_1 q_1 \\ t_2 = \theta_1 q_1 + \theta_2(q_2^* - q_1) \end{cases}$$

We can then substitute these values in the expression of the Principal's profit and solve

$$\max_{q_1} \left(\pi(\theta_1 q_1 - C(q_1)) - (1 - \pi)(\theta_2 - \theta_1)q_1 \right)$$

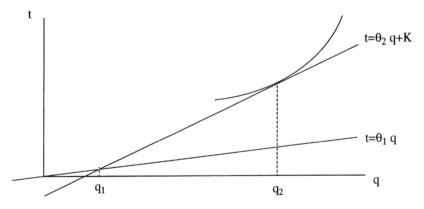

Figure 2.3
The second-best optimum

Note that the objective of this program consists of two terms. The first one is proportional to the social surplus[10] on type 1 and the second one represents the effect on incentive constraints on the seller's objective. Dividing by π, we see that the Principal should maximize

$$(\theta_1 q_1 - C(q_1)) - \frac{1 - \pi}{\pi}(\theta_2 - \theta_1)q_1$$

which we can call the *virtual surplus*. We will see a similar formula in section 2.3. The difference between the social surplus and the virtual surplus comes from the fact that when the Principal increases q_1, he makes the type 1 package more alluring to type 2; to prevent type 2 from choosing the contract designated for type 1, he must therefore reduce t_2 and thus decrease his own profits.

We finally get

$$C'(q_1) = \theta_1 - \frac{1 - \pi}{\pi}(\theta_2 - \theta_1) < \theta_1$$

so that $q_1 < q_1^*$: the quality sold to the coarse consumers is subefficient.[11]

The optimal mechanism has five properties that are common to all discrete-type models and can usually be taken for granted, thus making the resolution of the model much easier:

- The highest type gets an efficient allocation.

- Each type but the lowest is indifferent between his contract and that of the immediately lower type.

---

10. That is, the sum of the objectives of the Principal and the type 1 Agent. Note that we do not have to worry about the social surplus derived from selling to Agent 2, since we know that we implement the first-best $q_2 = q_2^*$.

11. If the proportion of coarse consumers π is low, the above formula will give a negative $C'(q_1)$; in that case it is optimal for the seller to propose a single contract designed for the sophisticated consumers. A more general treatment should obviously take this possibility into account from the start. Here this *exclusion* phenomenon can be prevented by assuming that π is high enough; we will see in section 3.2.4 that this is not possible when the Agent's characteristic is multidimensional.

- All types but the lowest type get a positive surplus: their *informational rent*, which increases with their type.
- All types but the highest type get a subefficient allocation.
- The lowest type gets zero surplus.

The informational rent is a central concept in adverse selection models. The Agent of type 2 gets it because he can always pretend his type is 1, consume quality q_1, and pay the price t_1, thus getting utility

$$\theta_2 q_1 - t_1$$

which is positive. On the other hand, type 1 does not gain anything by pretending to be type 2; this nets him utility

$$\theta_1 q_2 - t_2$$

which is negative. If there were n types of consumers $\theta_1 < \ldots < \theta_n$, each type $\theta_2, \ldots, \theta_n$ would get an informational rent, and this rent would increase from θ_2 to θ_n. Only the lowest type, θ_1, gets no rent.

Remark   By the taxation principle there is a nonlinear tariff that is equivalent to the optimal mechanism; it is simply

$$\begin{cases} t = t_1 & \text{if } q = q_1 \\ t = t_2 & \text{if } q = q_2 \\ t = \infty & \text{otherwise} \end{cases}$$

so the seller only proposes the two qualities required to segment the market.[12]

2.3   The Standard Model

The model I describe in this section sums up reasonably well the general features of adverse selection models. It introduces a Princi-

---

12. Such an extremely nonlinear tariff is less reasonable when the variable q is a quantity index, as it is in the price discrimination problem studied by Maskin-Riley (1984). Then it is sometimes possible to implement the optimum mechanism by using a menu of linear tariffs (see Rogerson 1987 for a necessary and sufficient condition).

pal and an Agent who exchange a vector of goods q and a monetary transfer p. The Agent has a characteristic θ that constitutes his private information. The utilities of both parties are given by

$$\begin{cases} W(q, t) & \text{for the Principal} \\ U(q, t, \theta) & \text{for the Agent of type } \theta \end{cases}$$

When the contract is signed, the Agent knows his type θ.[13] The Principal entertains an a priori belief on the Agent's type that is embodied in a probability distribution f with cumulative distribution function F on Θ which we will call his *prior*. Thus the Agent has a continuous set of possible types; this makes the graphical analysis used in section 2.2 impossible but will allow us to use differential techniques.

From the revelation principle we already know that the Principal just has to offer the Agent a menu of contracts $(q(.), t(.))$ indexed by an announcement of the Agent's type θ that must be truthful at the equilibrium. We thus need to characterize the menus of contracts such that

(IC) Agent θ chooses the $(q(\theta), t(\theta))$ that the Principal designed for him,

(IR) he thus obtains a utility level at least as large as his reservation utility, meaning what he could obtain by trading elsewhere (his second-best opportunity),

and the menu of contracts $(q(.), t(.))$ maximizes the expected utility of the Principal among all menus that satisfy (IR) and (IC).

Remarks

• As in section 2.2, the acronyms (IR) and (IC) come from the terms *individual rationality* and *incentive compatibility*.

• I abstract from the fact that as already noted in section 2.2.4, it may be optimal for the Principal to exclude some types θ from the

---

13. In some situations, it would be more reasonable to assume that the Agent only learns his type some time after the contract is signed but before its provisions are executed. I study this variant of the standard model in section 3.2.3.

exchange by denying them a contract (or at least falling back on a prior "no trade" contract).

· We could reinterpret this model by assuming that the Principal faces a population of Agents whose types are drawn from the cumulative distribution function F; this case is isomorphic to that we study here, with a single Agent whose type is random in the Principal's view. Many papers oscillate between the two interpretations, and so will I here.

2.3.1   Analysis of the Incentive Constraints

Let $V(\theta, \hat{\theta})$ be the utility achieved by an Agent of type θ who announces his type as $\hat{\theta}$ and therefore receives utility

$$V(\theta, \hat{\theta}) = U(q(\hat{\theta}), t(\hat{\theta}), \theta)$$

The mechanism (q, t) satisfies the incentive constraints if and only if being truthful brings every type of Agent at least as much utility as any kind of lie:

$$\forall (\theta, \hat{\theta}) \in \Theta^2, \quad V(\theta, \theta) \geq V(\theta, \hat{\theta}) \qquad (IC)$$

To simplify notation, I will assume from now on that q is one-dimensional. More important, I will take Θ to be a real interval[14] $[\underline{\theta}, \overline{\theta}]$ and let the Agent's utility function take the following form:

$$U(q, t, \theta) = u(q, \theta) - t$$

This presumes a quasi-linearity that implies that the Agent's marginal utility for money is constant; it simplifies some technical points, but mainly allows us to use surplus analysis.

I will also assume that the mechanism (q, t) is differentiable enough. It is sometimes possible to justify this assumption rigorously

---

14. The problem becomes much more complex, and the solution has very different properties when θ is multidimensional; see section 3.2.4.

by proving that the optimal mechanism indeed is at least piecewise differentiable.

For (q, t) to be incentive compatible, it must be that the following first- and second-order necessary conditions hold:[15]

$$\forall \theta \in \Theta, \quad \begin{cases} \dfrac{\partial V}{\partial \hat{\theta}}(\theta, \theta) = 0 \\[2ex] \dfrac{\partial^2 V}{\partial \hat{\theta}^2}(\theta, \theta) \leq 0 \end{cases}$$

The first-order condition boils down to

$$\frac{dt}{d\theta}(\theta) = \frac{\partial u}{\partial q}(q(\theta), \theta) \frac{dq}{d\theta}(\theta) \qquad (IC_1)$$

As to the second-order condition, that is,

$$\frac{d^2 t}{d\theta^2}(\theta) \geq \frac{\partial^2 u}{\partial q^2}(q(\theta), \theta) \left(\frac{dq}{d\theta}(\theta) \right)^2 + \frac{\partial u}{\partial q}(q(\theta), \theta) \frac{d^2 q}{d\theta^2}(\theta) \qquad (IC_2)$$

it can be simplified by differentiating (IC_1), which gives

$$\frac{d^2 t}{d\theta^2}(\theta) = \frac{\partial^2 u}{\partial q^2}(q(\theta), \theta) \left(\frac{dq}{d\theta}(\theta) \right)^2 + \frac{\partial u}{\partial q \partial \theta}(q(\theta), \theta) \frac{dq}{d\theta}(\theta)$$
$$+ \frac{\partial u}{\partial q}(q(\theta), \theta) \frac{d^2 q}{d\theta^2}(\theta)$$

whence by substituting into (IC_2),

$$\frac{\partial^2 u}{\partial q \partial \theta}(q(\theta), \theta) \frac{dq}{d\theta}(\theta) \geq 0$$

The first- and second-order necessary incentive conditions thus can be written as

---

15. These conditions are clearly not sufficient in general; however, we will soon see that they are sufficient in some circumstances.

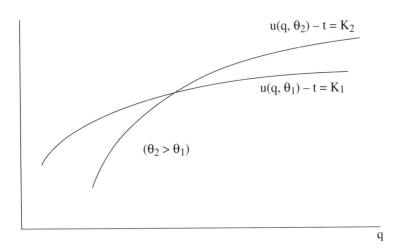

Figure 2.4
The Spence-Mirrlees condition

$$
\forall \theta \in \Theta, \quad
\begin{cases}
\dfrac{dt}{d\theta}(\theta) = \dfrac{\partial u}{\partial q}(q(\theta), \theta)\dfrac{dq}{d\theta}(\theta) & (IC_1) \\[2ex]
\dfrac{\partial^2 u}{\partial q\partial\theta}(q(\theta), \theta)\dfrac{dq}{d\theta}(\theta) \geq 0 & (IC_2)
\end{cases}
$$

Most models used in the literature simplify the analysis by assuming that the cross-derivative $\partial^2 u/\partial q\partial\theta$ has a constant sign. This is called the Spence-Mirrlees condition. I will assume that this derivative is positive:

$$
\forall\theta, \forall q, \quad \frac{\partial^2 u}{\partial q\partial\theta}(q, \theta) > 0
$$

This condition is also called the *single-crossing condition*; it indeed implies that the indifference curves of two different types can only cross once,[16] as is shown in figure 2.4 (where, for the sake of concreteness, I take u to be increasing and concave in q).

---

16. The simplest way to see this is to remark that for a given q where they cross, the indifference curves of different types are ordered: Higher types have steeper indifference curves, since the slopes $\partial u/\partial q$ increase with θ.

The Spence-Mirrlees condition has an economic content; it means that higher types (those Agents with a higher θ) are willing to pay more for a given increase in q than lower types. We may thus hope that we will be able to separate the different types of Agents by offering larger allocations q to higher types and making them pay for the privilege. This explains why the Spence-Mirrlees condition is also called the *sorting condition*, as it may allow us to sort through the different types of the Agent.

Let us now show that q belongs to a direct truthful mechanism (q, t) if and only if q is nondecreasing.[17] To see this, consider

$$\frac{\partial V}{\partial \hat{\theta}}(\theta, \hat{\theta}) = \frac{\partial u}{\partial q}(q(\hat{\theta}), \theta)\frac{dq}{d\theta}(\hat{\theta}) - \frac{dt}{d\theta}(\hat{\theta})$$

By writing (IC_1) in $\hat{\theta}$, we get

$$\frac{\partial u}{\partial q}(q(\hat{\theta}), \hat{\theta})\frac{dq}{d\theta}(\hat{\theta}) = \frac{dt}{d\theta}(\hat{\theta})$$

whence

$$\frac{\partial V}{\partial \hat{\theta}}(\theta, \hat{\theta}) = \left(\frac{\partial u}{\partial q}(q(\hat{\theta}), \theta) - \frac{\partial u}{\partial q}(q(\hat{\theta}), \hat{\theta})\right)\frac{dq}{d\theta}(\hat{\theta})$$

But the sign of the right-hand side is that of

$$\frac{\partial^2 u}{\partial q \partial \theta}(q(\hat{\theta}), \theta^*)\,(\theta - \hat{\theta})\frac{dq}{d\theta}(\hat{\theta})$$

for some θ^* that lies between θ and $\hat{\theta}$. Given the Spence-Mirrlees condition, this term has the same sign as $(\theta - \hat{\theta})$ if q is nondecreasing. Thus the function $\hat{\theta} \to V(\theta, \hat{\theta})$ increases until $\hat{\theta} = \theta$ and then decreases. Therefore $\hat{\theta} = \theta$ is the global maximizer of $V(\theta, \hat{\theta})$.

This is a very remarkable result. We started with the (doubly infinite in number) global incentive constraints (IC) and the Spence-

17. If we had assumed the Spence-Mirrlees condition with $\partial^2 u/\partial q \partial \theta < 0$, then q should be nonincreasing.

Mirrlees condition allowed us to transform them into the much simpler local conditions (IC_1) and (IC_2) without any loss of generality. Note how the problem separates nicely: (IC_2) requires that q should be non-decreasing and (IC_1) gives us the associated t. This will be very useful in solving the model. If the Spence-Mirrlees condition did not hold, the study of the incentive problem would have to be global and therefore much more complex.[18]

2.3.2 Solving the Model

Let us go on analyzing this model with a continuous set of types. I will neglect technicalities in the following; in particular, I will assume that all differential equations can safely be integrated.[19] I will assume that the Principal's utility function is quasi-separable and is

$$t - C(q)$$

I will also assume that

$$\forall q, \theta \quad \frac{\partial u}{\partial \theta}(q, \theta) > 0$$

meaning that a given allocation gives the higher types a higher utility level. Finally, I will assume that the Spence-Mirrlees condition holds:

$$\forall \theta, \forall q, \quad \frac{\partial^2 u}{\partial q \partial \theta}(q, \theta) > 0$$

Let $v(\theta)$ denote the utility the Agent of type θ gets at the optimum of his program. As the optimal mechanism is truthful, we get

$$v(\theta) = V(\theta, \theta) = u(q(\theta), \theta) - t(\theta)$$

---

18. A few papers (e.g., Moore 1988) adopt a "nonlocal" approach that does not rely on the Spence-Mirrlees condition; this typically assumes that only the downward incentive constraints bind. Also Milgrom-Shannon (1994) link the Spence-Mirrlees condition and the theory of supermodular functions.
19. More rigorous-minded readers should turn to Guesnerie-Laffont (1984) for a complete analysis.

and (IC_1) implies that

$$\frac{dv}{d\theta}(\theta) = \frac{\partial u}{\partial \theta}(q(\theta), \theta)$$

which we have assumed is positive. The utility $v(\theta)$ represents the *informational rent* of the Agent; the equation above shows that this rent is an increasing function of his type. Higher types thus benefit more from their private information. Indeed, type θ can always pretend his type is $\hat{\theta} < \theta$; he would thus obtain a utility

$$u(q(\hat{\theta}), \theta) - t(\hat{\theta}) = v(\hat{\theta}) + u(q(\hat{\theta}), \theta) - u(q(\hat{\theta}), \hat{\theta})$$

which is larger than $v(\hat{\theta})$ since u increases in θ. The ability of higher types to "hide behind" lower types is responsible for their informational rent.[20] This rent is the price the Principal has to pay for higher types to reveal their information.

In most applications the individual rationality constraint is taken to be independent of the Agent's type.[21] This amounts to assuming that the Agent's private information is only relevant in his relationship with the Principal. Under this assumption, which is not innocuous,[22] we can normalize the Agent's reservation utility to 0 and write his individual rationality constraint as

$$\forall \theta, \quad v(\theta) \geq 0 \qquad (IR)$$

Given that v is increasing, the individual rationality constraint (IR) boils down to

$$v(\underline{\theta}) \geq 0$$

which must actually be an equality, since transfers are costly for the Principal.

---

20. Note that on the contrary, lower types have no incentive to hide behind higher types.
21. We will see an important exception in section 3.1.3.
22. See Jullien (1995) for a general analysis of the adverse selection problem when reservation utilities are allowed to depend on types in a nonrestricted way.

These preliminary computations allow us to eliminate the transfers $t(\theta)$ from the problem; indeed, we have

$$v(\theta) = \int_{\underline{\theta}}^{\theta} \frac{\partial u}{\partial \theta}(q(\tau), \tau)d\tau$$

whence

$$t(\theta) = u(q(\theta), \theta) - v(\theta)$$
$$= u(q(\theta), \theta) - \int_{\underline{\theta}}^{\theta} \frac{\partial u}{\partial \theta}(q(\tau), \tau)d\tau$$

Let us now return to the Principal's objective[23]

$$\int_{\underline{\theta}}^{\overline{\theta}} \left(t(\theta) - C(q(\theta)) \right) f(\theta)d\theta$$

Substituting for t, it can be rewritten as

$$\int_{\underline{\theta}}^{\overline{\theta}} \left(u(q(\theta), \theta) - \int_{\underline{\theta}}^{\theta} \frac{\partial u}{\partial \theta}(q(\tau), \tau)d\tau - C(q(\theta)) \right) f(\theta)d\theta$$

Let us define the *hazard rate*

$$h(\theta) = \frac{f(\theta)}{1 - F(\theta)}$$

This definition is borrowed from the statistical literature on duration data:[24] if $F(\theta)$ were the probability of dying before age θ, then $h(\theta)$ would represent the instantaneous probability of dying at age θ provided that one has survived until then.

Now applying Fubini's theorem[25] or simply integrating by parts, the Principal's objective becomes

---

23. Recall that f is the probability distribution function and F the cumulative distribution function of the Principal's prior on Θ.
24. Some economists improperly define the hazard rate as $1/h(\theta)$.
25. Recall that Fubini's theorem states that if f is integrable on $[a, b] \times [c, d]$, then

$$\int_a^b \int_c^d f(x, y)dxdy = \int_a^b \left(\int_c^d f(x, y)dy \right)dx = \int_c^d \left(\int_a^b f(x, y)dx \right)dy$$

$$I = \int_{\underline{\theta}}^{\overline{\theta}} H(q(\theta), \theta) f(\theta) d\theta$$

where

$$H(q, \theta) = u(q, \theta) - C(q) - \frac{\partial u}{\partial \theta}(q, \theta) \frac{1}{h(\theta)}$$

The function $H(q(\theta), \theta)$ is the virtual surplus. It consists of two terms; the first one,

$$u(q(\theta), \theta) - C(q(\theta))$$

is the first-best social surplus,[26] namely the sum of the utilities of the Principal and the type θ Agent. The second term $-v'(\theta)/h(\theta)$ therefore measures the impact of the incentive problem on the social surplus. This term originates in the necessity of keeping the informational rent $v(\theta)$ increasing: If type θ's allocation is increased, then so is his informational rent, and to maintain incentive compatibility, the Principal must also increase the rents of all types $\theta' > \theta$ who are in proportion $1 - F(\theta)$.

We still need to take into account the second-order incentive constraint

$$\frac{dq}{d\theta}(\theta) \geq 0$$

The simplest way to proceed is to neglect this constraint in a first attempt; the (presumed) solution then is obtained by maximizing the integrand of I in every point, whence

$$\frac{\partial H}{\partial q}(q^*(\theta), \theta) = 0$$

Writing this equation in full, we have

---

26. It is legitimate to speak of surplus here, since the transfers have a constant marginal utility equal to one for both Principal and Agent.

$$\frac{\partial u}{\partial q}(q^*(\theta), \theta) = C'(q^*(\theta)) + \frac{\partial^2 u}{\partial q \partial \theta}(q^*(\theta), \theta)\frac{1}{h(\theta)}$$

Note that the left-hand side of this equation has the dimension of a price; in fact it is just the inverse demand function of Agent θ. Since we assumed that the cross-derivative is positive, this equation therefore tells us that price is greater than marginal cost; the difference between them is the source of the informational rent, and it also represents the deviation from the first-best.

The Separating Optimum

If the function q^* is nondecreasing, it is the optimum. We can then say that types are separated, and revelation is perfect, as in figure 2.5.

Higher types θ have a larger allocation q, and they pay more for it. Note that it is often possible to make assumptions that guarantee this separation result. If, for instance, $u(q, \theta) = \theta q$ and C is convex, then the reader should check that assuming that the hazard rate h is nondecreasing is sufficient to imply that q^* is increasing. The literature often resorts to such an assumption, since it is satisfied by many usual probability distributions.

*The Bunching Optimum

If the function q^* happens to be decreasing on a subinterval, then it cannot be the solution. It is then necessary to take into account the

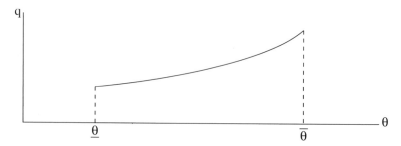

Figure 2.5
A separating optimum

constraint that q should be nondecreasing, which means that we must resort to optimal control theory. Since I do not think that optimal control theory should be a prerequisite for reading this book, I will give a self-contained analysis below, using only elementary notions. Those readers who prefer a more direct treatment should refer to Laffont (1989, 10) and to Kamien-Schwartz (1981), for instance, for the basics of optimal control theory. First, we note that the solution will consist of subintervals in which q is increasing and subintervals in which it is constant. Now we take a subinterval $[\theta_1, \theta_2]$ in which q is increasing and $\partial H / \partial q$ is positive. Then we can add a positive infinitesimal function $dq(\theta)$ to $q(\theta)$ in that subinterval so that $dq(\theta_1) = dq(\theta_2) = 0$ and $(q + dq)$ stays increasing. This clearly increases H on $[\theta_1, \theta_2]$ and thus improves the objective of the Principal. A similar argument applies when $\partial H / \partial q$ is negative on a subinterval where q is increasing. Thus whenever q is increasing, the solution must satisfy $\partial H / \partial q = 0$, which is just to say that it must coincide with q^*.

The determination of the subintervals where q is constant is a bit trickier. Take such a (maximal) subinterval $[\theta_1, \theta_2]$; on this subinterval the solution must equal a constant $\tilde{q}$ such that $q^*(\theta_1) = q^*(\theta_2) = \tilde{q}$. This defines two functions $\theta_1(\tilde{q})$ and $\theta_2(\tilde{q})$. We just have to determine the value of $\tilde{q}$. Now let

$$F(q) = \int_{\theta_1(q)}^{\theta_2(q)} \frac{\partial H}{\partial q}(q, \theta)d\theta,$$

and assume that $F(\tilde{q}) > 0$. Then add to the solution an infinitesimal positive constant on $[\theta_1, \theta_2]$ (and a smaller, decreasing amount on $[\theta_2, \theta_2 + \varepsilon]$, where $q^*(\theta_2 + \varepsilon) = \tilde{q} + dq$). The Principal's objective will be unchanged on $[\theta_2, \theta_2 + \varepsilon]$ since $\partial H / \partial q = 0$ there by assumption. However, it will increase by $F(\tilde{q})dq$ on $[\theta_1, \theta_2]$. This, and a similar reasoning when $F(\tilde{q}) < 0$, prove that we must have $F(\tilde{q}) = 0$. But since $\partial H / \partial q = 0$ in θ_1 and θ_2, it is easily seen that the derivative of F is

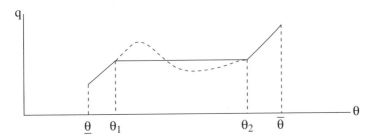

Figure 2.6
An optimum with bunching

$$F'(q) = \int_{\theta_1(q)}^{\theta_2(q)} \frac{\partial^2 H}{\partial q^2}(q, \theta)d\theta$$

Thus if we make the reasonable assumption that the virtual surplus is concave in q,[27] $\partial^2 H/\partial q^2$ will be negative and therefore F will be decreasing. This implies that if there is a $\tilde{q}$ such that $F(\tilde{q}) = 0$, then it is unique, which completes our characterization of the solution.

The solution in this more complicated case is depicted in figure 2.6. We then speak of "bunching" or "pooling" of types on the subintervals where q is constant, and there is less than perfect revelation. Obviously all the types $\theta \in [\theta_1, \theta_2]$ pay the same transfer t for their constant allocation.

Exercises

Exercise 2.1

Assume that there are n types of consumers in the wine-selling example of section 2.2 and that $\theta_1 < \ldots < \theta_n$. Their respective prior probabilities are $\pi_1, \ldots, \pi_n$, with $\sum_{i=1}^{n}\pi_i = 1$. Show that the only binding constraints are the downward adjacent incentive constraints

---

27. Assume, for instance, that u is concave in q, C is convex and that $\partial^2 u/\partial q^2$ increases in θ.

$$\theta_i q_i - t_i \geq \theta_i q_{i-1} - t_{i-1}$$

for $i = 2, \ldots, n$ and the individual rationality constraint of the lowest type

$$\theta_1 q_1 - t_1 \geq 0$$

Exercise 2.2

In the context of 2.3.2, assume that $u(q, \theta) = \theta q$ and C is convex.

1. Show that a necessary and sufficient condition for q^* to be increasing is that $\theta - 1/h(\theta)$ be increasing.

2. A function g is *log-concave* iff log g is concave. Show that all concave functions are log-concave. Show that if $(1 - F)$ is log-concave, then q^* is increasing.

3. Show that q^* is increasing if θ is uniformly distributed.

4. A bit more tricky: Show that if f is log-concave, then so is $(1 - F)$.

5. Conclude that q^* is increasing if θ is normally distributed.

Exercise 2.3 (difficult)

My characterization of the bunching optimum in section 2.3.2 seems to rely on a hidden assumption: that bunching does not occur "at the bottom" (on some interval $[\underline{\theta}, \theta_1]$) or "at the top" (on some interval $[\theta_2, \overline{\theta}]$). Can you modify the proof so that it also covers these two cases?

References

Guesnerie, R., and J.-J. Laffont. 1984. A complete solution to a class of principal-agent problems with an application to the control of a self-managed firm. *Journal of Public Economics.* 25:329–69.

Jullien, B. 1995. Participation constraints in adverse selection models. Mimeo CREST.

Kamien, M., and N. Schwartz. 1981. *Dynamic Optimization: The Calculus of Variations and Optimal Control in Economics and Management.* Amsterdam: North-Holland.

Kamien, M., and N. Schwartz. 1981. *Dynamic Optimization: The Calculus of Variations and Optimal Control in Economics and Management.* Amsterdam: North-Holland.

Laffont, J.-J. 1989. *The Economics of Uncertainty and Information.* Cambridge: MIT Press.

Maskin, E., and J. Riley. 1984. Monopoly with incomplete information. *Rand Journal of Economics* 15:171–96.

Milgrom, P., and C. Shannon. 1994. Monotone comparative statics. *Econometrica* 62:157–80.

Moore, J. 1988. Contracts between two parties with private information. *Review of Economic Studies* 55:49–70.

Moore, J. 1992. Implementation, contracts, and renegotiation in environments with complete information. In *Advances in Economic Theory,* vol. 1, J. J. Laffont ed. Cambridge: Cambridge University Press.

Mussa, M., and S. Rosen. 1978. Monopoly and product quality. *Journal of Economic Theory* 18:301–17.

Rogerson, W. 1987. On the optimality of menus of linear contracts. Mimeo. Northwestern University.

Stiglitz, J., and A. Weiss. 1981. Credit rationing in markets with imperfect information. *American Economic Review* 71:393–410.

3

Adverse Selection: Examples and Extensions

This chapter studies shows how the theory presented in the previous chapter can be applied to various economic problems. It also presents some of its main extensions.

3.1 Examples of Applications

3.1.1 Regulating a Firm

In modern economies an important part of production is carried out by firms that are natural monopolies[1] in their industry. This is arguably the case in the energy sector and the transportation sector, for instance. The government must then regulate these firms so that they do not behave as monopolies, be they public or private. The main difficulty involved is that regulators typically don't know many of the characteristics of the firm. Much of the literature has focused since the seminal paper by Baron-Myerson

---

1. For the sake of this discussion, just define a natural monopoly as a firm with subadditive costs:

$$\forall n, \forall (q_1, \ldots, q_n), \quad C\left(\sum_{i=1}^{n} q_i\right) < \sum_{i=1}^{n} C(q_i)$$

so that for purely technical reasons, it is socially efficient to set up the firm as a monopoly. Natural monopolies are connected with the presence of strong increasing returns and are often said to arise in industries with large fixed costs due to the importance of infrastructures, for instance, utilities and transportation.

(1982) on the case where the firm is better informed of its costs than the regulator.

Let us consider a firm that produces a marketed good for which demand is given by an inverse demand function $P(q)$. The cost of producing q units of the good is $C(q, \theta)$. The parameter θ is private information of the firm; however, its production is observable. The firm is regulated by a public agency who gives it transfers t conditional on its production level. The objective of the regulator is to maximize social surplus, a weighted sum of the firm's profit $(t + P(q)q - C(q, \theta))$ and consumer surplus $(S(q) - P(q)q - t)$, where

$$S(q) = \int_0^q P(c)dc$$

The weights given to consumer surplus and profit depend on the regulator's redistributive objectives and are summed up in a coefficient k: one dollar of profit is socially worth as much as k dollars of consumer surplus. Moreover public transfers involve direct costs (e.g., the cost of tax collection) and economic distortions (since transfers are typically not lump-sum) that jointly define the opportunity cost of public funds. It is therefore reasonable to assume that any transfer t occasions a social cost λt, so that social surplus is

$$W = k(t + P(q)q - C(q, \theta)) + S(q) - P(q)q - t - \lambda t$$

The regulator must find a direct truthful mechanism $(q(\theta), t(\theta))$ that maximizes the expectation of W (taken over all possible cost parameters θ) while giving each type of firm a nonnegative profit.

This model differs from the standard model in that W depends on θ through the Agent's utility function; however, the techniques used to solve it and the qualitative results obtained are quite similar. Therefore I will not solve the model here. The reader should consult the survey by Caillaud-Guesnerie-Rey-Tirole (1988) or the useful perspective given by Laffont (1994).

I should note here that Laffont-Tirole (1986) introduced a somewhat different model in which the firm's costs C depend on both an efficiency parameter and an effort level, both of which are unobserved by the regulator, and the costs can be (imperfectly) observed. They show that the optimal incentive scheme then takes the form of offering the firm a menu of linear schemes $t = a + bC$, where there are as many (appropriately chosen) (a, b) pairs as there are efficiency parameters. The most efficient firms choose a fixed-price contract (a linear scheme with a zero b), and less efficient firms choose a linear scheme with a higher b. Thus the solution prescribes *price-cap* contracts only for the most efficient firms; the less efficient a firm is, the more its contract will look like a *cost-plus* contract. These two popular regulatory proposals therefore are justified and generalized within the context of the Laffont-Tirole model. I should note here that the Bible in this field, the book by Laffont-Tirole (1993), is essentially based on this model.

3.1.2   Optimal Taxation

Consider an economy populated by consumers-producers indexed by a parameter θ distributed according to a probability distribution function f on $[\underline{\theta}, \overline{\theta}]$; all individuals have the same utility function

$$U(C) - L$$

where C denotes consumption, L denotes labor, and U is increasing and concave. An individual of parameter θ has a constant-returns-to-scale production function given by

$$Q = \theta L$$

so that θ is the productivity of this individual.

Note that in the autarkic economy where each agent consumes the product of his own labor, consumption will be given by

$$U'(C) = \frac{1}{\theta}$$

and utility increases with θ, as should be expected.

The government wants to implement an allocation of consumption and labor $(L(\theta), C(\theta))$ that maximizes social welfare. I will assume this is given by the utilitarian criterion[2]

$$\int_{\underline{\theta}}^{\overline{\theta}} \Big(U(C(\theta)) - L(\theta) \Big) f(\theta) d\theta$$

The government must of course take into account a scarcity constraint that implies that the economy cannot consume more than it produces:

$$\int_{\underline{\theta}}^{\overline{\theta}} C(\theta) f(\theta) d\theta \leq \int_{\underline{\theta}}^{\overline{\theta}} Q(\theta) f(\theta) d\theta$$

If the government can observe individual productivities θ, things are pretty simple: The government must first choose a production level that balances the utility of consumption and the disutility of labor; then he can put the more productive agents to work and the less productive to rest, and finally share production equally between all agents. This first-best "solution" has the striking feature that utility *decreases* in θ, since the less productive individuals do not work but consume as much as the more productive agents.

Of course real-life governments have very little information on individual productivities. The only thing they can do is use taxation systems that rely on observable variables. Labor inputs are typically unobserved by the government; on the other hand, production can reasonably be taken as observable. Thus the government must rely on a tax on production to achieve his goals.

This model fits almost exactly within the standard model studied in the previous chapter: A tax on production can be assimilated to a

---

2. This nonweighted choice implies that redistributive objectives are left out of the model.

nonlinear tariff $C = c(Q)$. We just have to find a direct truthful mechanism $(Q(\theta), C(\theta))$ that maximizes social welfare under the scarcity constraint. The only new feature of this model is that there is no individual rationality constraint, since agents cannot refuse taxation (barring tax evasion). On the other hand, we now have a scarcity constraint whose integral form differentiates this model from the standard model and justifies that we solve it here.

First note that the utility of individual θ, rewritten as a function of the variables of the "contract," is proportional to

$$\theta U(C) - Q$$

The results we obtained in section 2.3.1 thus apply directly (replacing q with C and t with Q); they show that the mechanism $(Q(\theta), C(\theta))$ is incentive compatible if and only if

$$\begin{cases} Q'(\theta) = \theta U'(C(\theta))C'(\theta) & (IC_1) \\ C'(\theta) \geq 0 & (IC_2) \end{cases}$$

Note that if $V(\theta)$ is the utility $(U(C(\theta)) - Q(\theta)/\theta)$ achieved by the individual of productivity θ, this implies that

$$V'(\theta) = \frac{Q(\theta)}{\theta^2}$$

and thus utility must increase in θ for a mechanism to be incentive compatible, which obviously rules out the first-best solution.

The objective of the government therefore is to maximize

$$\int_{\underline{\theta}}^{\overline{\theta}} \left(U(C(\theta)) - \frac{Q(\theta)}{\theta} \right) f(\theta)d\theta$$

under the scarcity constraint and the first- and second-order incentive constraints. As in section 2.3.2, we will proceed by eliminating one of the two variables, here $Q(\theta)$. To do this, note that by integrating by parts the first-order incentive constraint, we get

$$Q(\theta) = K + \theta U(C(\theta)) - \int_{\underline{\theta}}^{\theta} U(C(t))dt$$

The scarcity constraint, which must be an equality since U is increasing, then gives us

$$\int_{\underline{\theta}}^{\bar{\theta}} C(\theta) f(\theta) d\theta = K + \int_{\underline{\theta}}^{\bar{\theta}} \left(\theta U(C(\theta)) - \int_{\underline{\theta}}^{\theta} U(C(t)) dt \right) f(\theta) d\theta$$

Letting $F(\theta) = \int_{\underline{\theta}}^{\theta} f(t) dt$ and using Fubini's theorem, we get

$$K = \int_{\underline{\theta}}^{\bar{\theta}} \left(C(\theta) f(\theta) - \theta U(C(\theta)) f(\theta) + (1 - F(\theta)) U(C(\theta)) \right) d\theta$$

which completes the elimination of $Q(\theta)$. There just remains to maximize the government's objective, which simplifies since

$$U(C(\theta)) - \frac{Q(\theta)}{\theta} = \frac{1}{\theta} \int_{\underline{\theta}}^{\theta} U(C(t)) dt - \frac{K}{\theta}$$

The simplest approach, as in section 2.3.2, consists in ignoring the second-order constraint $C'(\theta) \geq 0$ at first; denoting $M(\theta) = \int_{\theta}^{\bar{\theta}} f(t)/t \, dt$ and using Fubini's theorem again, the government's objective becomes

$$\int_{\underline{\theta}}^{\bar{\theta}} M(\theta) U(C(\theta)) d\theta - KM(\underline{\theta})$$

or, substituting the expression of K,

$$\int_{\underline{\theta}}^{\bar{\theta}} \Big(M(\theta) U(C(\theta)) - M(\underline{\theta}) \Big(C(\theta) f(\theta) - \theta U(C(\theta)) f(\theta)$$
$$+ (1 - F(\theta)) U(C(\theta)) \Big) \Big) d\theta$$

Maximizing this integral in every point gives

$$U'(C^*(\theta)) = \frac{M(\underline{\theta}) f(\theta)}{M(\theta) + M(\underline{\theta}) f(\theta) \theta - M(\underline{\theta})(1 - F(\theta))}$$

The function C^* is increasing if and only if the right-hand-side term is decreasing in θ. If such is the case, then C^* is the solution and the tax schedule is obtained by solving for the associated $Q(\theta)$. Otherwise, there must be a bunching phenomenon: Some interval of consumers will get the same allocation (Q, C). Outside this interval the solution coincides with C^*. As a technical aside, it is easily seen that the solution in C^* (but not in Q) coincides with the autarkic solution at both ends (in $\underline{\theta}$ and $\overline{\theta}$) and is lower everywhere else; this is typical of continuous type models with an integral constraint.

Lollivier-Rochet (1983) study a similar model but introduce redistributive objectives. They show that the bunching phenomenon only concerns the less productive agents and appears when the government values redistribution strongly enough. Their paper is also of interest because it solves the model using more advanced but much more elegant techniques than those I used here.

Optimal taxation is a very large field, and I cannot do it justice here. The reader can turn to Mirrlees (1986) for an authoritative survey.

3.1.3 The Insurer as a Monopolist

We will study in this subsection the problem facing an insurer who is a monopoly and serves a population that contains several risk classes.[3] I will assume that all individuals in this population are identical, as far as observable characteristics are concerned: If, for instance, the contract we analyze insures against the risk of invalidity, the population under study only contains forty-year-old males living in Boston who do office work and who have not had heart trouble. However, there remains elements of heterogeneity in the population: Each individual knows the state of his health better than the insurer does.[4] If the insurer only proposes a contract designed for the average risk in the population, he risks attracting

---

3. The analysis here is adapted from Stiglitz (1977); it differs from the more famous studies of the market for insurance in which firms are assumed to act competitively.
4. Alternatively, there may exist variables that are observable but that the law forbids insurers to use to compute the terms of the contract. This is often the case for ethical reasons.

only high-risk individuals, in which case the contract will make losses: This is where the term *adverse selection* comes from. Therefore the insurer should consider offering as many contracts as there are risk classes.

Let W denote the initial wealth of each Agent. The effect of an accident is to reduce this wealth by an amount d that represents the *pretium doloris*, the discounted loss of wages over the rest of the working life, and so on. An insurance contract consists of a premium q paid by the insurees and a reimbursement R that they receive upon having an accident. The final wealth therefore is

$$W_A = W - d - q + R$$

in case of an accident and

$$W_N = W - q$$

otherwise. The expected utility of an Agent is

$$U = pu(W_A) + (1 - p)u(W_N)$$

if he belongs to the risk class whose probability of having an accident is p; u is an increasing concave function. I will assume that two risk classes coexist in the population: the high risks, whose probability of having an accident is p_H, and the low risks, for which it is $p_L < p_H$.

First note that this model differs from the standard model in that the reservation utility of an Agent of class i is

$$p_i u(W - d) + (1 - p_i)u(W)$$

and this depends on his risk class, which is unknown to the insurer. This will turn out to have important consequences. Also the agent's utility is not quasi-separable in premium and reimbursement.

Even though this model is quite different from the standard model, a Spence-Mirrlees condition holds. The marginal rate of substitution between the premium and the reimbursement indeed is

$$-\frac{\partial U/\partial q}{\partial U/\partial R} = \frac{pu'(W_A) + (1-p)u'(W_N)}{pu'(W_A)}$$

which is a decreasing function of p. It should therefore be possible to separate the high risks from the low risks by offering them a better coverage in return for a higher premium.

The profit of the Principal (the insurer) depends on the risk class of the insuree[5] as well as on the contract:

$$\pi = q - pR$$

We will assume that the insurance company is risk-neutral; this is reasonable because insurance companies generally face many un-correlated risks. The first-best therefore consists in insuring completely every class of Agents so that their final wealths do not depend on the occurrence of an accident.

The analytical treatment of this model is more complicated than that of the standard model, since both reservation utilities and profits are type-dependent. However, it can be studied graphically by tracing indifference curves in the plane (W_N, W_A), where the 45-degree line corresponds to complete insurance (since wealth is the same whether or not an accident has happened), and point O, with coordinates $(W, W - d)$, represents the no insurance situation. It is easy to check that the indifference curves of the insurees are decreasing and convex. The slope of the indifference curve of risk class p is

$$-\frac{1-p}{p}\frac{u'(W_N)}{u'(W_A)}$$

and the indifference curve of low risks is steeper than that of high risks, which confirms the Spence-Mirrlees condition. Isoprofit curves are straight lines; the isoprofit line for a given risk class p has slope

---

5. This is another crucial difference with the standard model.

$$-\frac{1-p}{p}$$

and therefore is tangent to the indifference curve of that class on the complete insurance line. Note that utilities increase in figure 3.1 when going northeast and profits increase when going southwest.

The second-best optimum is obtained by looking for a pair of contracts $C_L = (q_L, R_L)$ and $C_H = (q_H, R_H)$ that maximize the expected profit of the Principal under the usual incentive constraints and that give each class at least as much utility as with no insurance. Again, solving this program analytically is difficult, but most properties of the solution can be obtained graphically.

At least one of the two risk classes must be indifferent between the contract that is designed for it and no insurance; otherwise, the insurer could increase the premia and reduce the reimbursements. It is easy to see from a figure that if C_L gives at least as much utility to the low risks as no insurance, then it must also be preferred to no insurance by the high risks; therefore the low risks must be indifferent between C_L and no insurance.

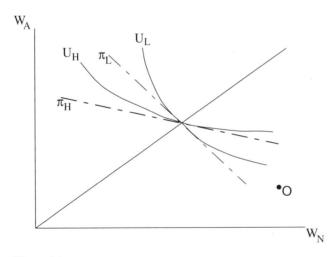

Figure 3.1
The insurance model

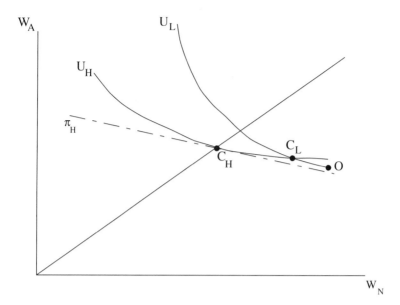

Figure 3.2
The optimal insurance contract

Again, a little playing with the figures should convince the reader that C_H gives maximal profits to the insurer when it is located in a point where the indifference curve of the high risks is tangent to the corresponding isoprofit line, but we know that this can only happen on the complete insurance line. Thus the high risks are completely insured, and we get figure 3.2, where again C_L is designed for low risks and C_H for high risks.

Unlike the low risks, the high risks are completely insured and receive an informational rent;[6] they are indifferent between C_L and C_H. As in the standard model the graphic analysis leaves one parameter to be determined: the location of C_H on the diagonal, or equivalently the

---

6. Note that in the standard model, one expects the "good" Agent to receive an informational rent. Here it seems natural to define the low risks as the "good" agents, but it is the high risks who get the rent, and so on. This apparent paradox is due to the peculiar features of the insurance problem, the most important being that this is a case of "common values": The probabilities p_i play a key role in both the Principal's and the Agent's objective functions.

location of C_L on the indifference curve between O and the complete insurance line. It is easy to see that in order to maximize profits, C_L must be closer to O when the proportion of high risks in the population increases. Indeed, Stiglitz (1977) shows that beyond a certain proportion of high risks, C_L will actually coincide with O so that the low risks get no insurance: Any contract that attracts them would also attract the high risks. This is of course a striking form of adverse selection: Only the high risks can find insurance! Note also that while it is clear from figure 3.2 that the insurer always makes positive profits on the low risks, this need not be the case with the high risks: When there are many low risks in the population, they will get almost complete insurance, and the insurer will make losses on the high risks.[7] In that case the low risks in effect cross-subsidize the high risks. Even though C_H makes losses in that configuration, there is nothing unstable in it: If the insurer were to withdraw C_H, the high risks would all buy the contract C_L, and this would make losses on them, thus depleting the insurer's profits.

3.1.4 Implicit Contracts

My final application concerns implicit contracts as a foundation stone for the study of business cycles and unemployment. This was a very active research area at the end of the 1970s and at the beginning of the 1980s, but very few macroeconomists would still consider it a promising field, for reasons that I will give below. Thus this section is mainly of historical interest.

The study of business cycles shows that the real wage varies little during the cycle, while employment is much more volatile. This stylized fact was observed long ago, but it is not easily explained by the main competing macroeconomic theories. The theory of implicit contracts is an attempt to provide such an explanation. It aims at describing how firms set real wages and employment through a

---

7. This is not the case on figure 3.2, since the π_H isoprofit line lies below O.

contract[8] with their employees. When prospects are uncertain, this contract must trade off optimal risk-sharing and productive efficiency. The contributors to this literature hoped that it would shed new light on the fluctuations of employment and wages.

Early models of implicit contracts took information to be symmetric; they showed that if the firm is less risk-averse than its employees, it will insure them by giving them a utility level that does not depend too much on the state of the world. Thus the theory can explain why wages vary little during the business cycle. On the other hand, it predicts efficient employment levels and therefore it cannot explain unemployment.

More recent models assumed that the firm acquires a better information on the state of the world than its employees after the contract is signed. If the firm is risk-averse, it will want to pay lower wages when the state of the world is unfavorable so as to share risks with its employees. However, the fact that employees do not observe the state of the world prevents the firm from lowering wages other than by reducing employment beyond what is efficient. Some contributions therefore obtained unemployment outcomes; I will present below such a model, due to Hart (1983). As a conclusion I will explain why this type of result is fragile.

The Model

Consider a firm that uses labor l to produce a good of price s, with a production function given by $x = g(l)$; g is increasing and strictly concave. The price of the good s is a random variable that can take two values $s_1 < s_2$ with respective probabilities π_1 and π_2 ($\pi_1 + \pi_2 = 1$). Let w be the total wages paid by the firm:[9] Its profit thus is $(sg(l) - w)$ and its utility[10] is the expectation of

---

8. There are very few such *explicit* contracts. This is the reason why Azariadis (1975) coined the term "implicit contracts," but that raises difficulties to which I will return later.
9. Not to be confused with the hourly wage w/l.
10. More accurately, that of its shareholders.

$V(sg(l) - w)$

where V is increasing and concave. To simplify things, I will assume that the firm has only one employee, whose utility is the expectation of

$U(w - Rl)$

when he works l hours and receives wages w (U is an increasing and concave function). The positive constant R measures the disutility of work (or, equivalently, the value of leisure) for the employee. Note that this utility function excludes income effects: the employee's labor supply does not depend on his income. The employee has outside opportunities that provide him with a reservation utility $\overline{U}$.

The model has two periods. At date 1, the firm and the employee sign a contract[11] which specifies employment and wages in each state of the world. At date 2, s is revealed and production takes place.

Finally, I will make the crucial assumption that neither the firm nor the employee have access to an insurance company that would cover the risks involved in their common productive activity.

The Symmetric Information Optimum
Assume here that s is equally unknown to both parties when the contract is signed. A contract then specifies employment (hours) and wages in each state of the world, as a list (l_1, w_1, l_2, w_2). The optimal contract is the solution of

$$\max_{(l_1, w_1, l_2, w_2)} \left(\pi_1 V(s_1 g(l_1) - w_1) + \pi_2 V(s_2 g(l_2) - w_2) \right)$$

given the employee's participation constraint (IR):

$$\pi_1 U(w_1 - Rl_1) + \pi_2 U(w_2 - Rl_2) \geq \overline{U}$$

---

11. Which, as in almost all of the literature, I will take to be explicit.

Let λ be the multiplier associated with the employee's participation constraint. Differentiating the Lagrangian with respect to l_1 and w_1 gives

$$s_1 V'(s_1 g(l_1) - w_1) g'(l_1) = \lambda R U'(w_1 - Rl_1)$$
$$V'(s_1 g(l_1) - w_1) = \lambda U'(w_1 - Rl_1)$$

and we can write two similar equations for the differentiation with respect to l_2 and w_2, whence

$$s_1 g'(l_1) = s_2 g'(l_2) = R$$

and

$$\frac{V'(s_1 g(l_1) - w_1)}{U'(w_1 - Rl_1)} = \frac{V'(s_2 g(l_2) - w_2)}{U'(w_2 - Rl_2)}$$

The first of these two equations reflects the productive efficiency of the contract: The global surplus $(s_i g(l) - Rl)$ is maximized in each state of the world i, even though employment is of course higher in state 2 than in state 1. I will denote by l_1^* and l_2^* the corresponding efficient employment levels. The second equation describes optimal risk-sharing, with the ratio of marginal utilities independent of the state of the world.

Take the special case where the firm is risk-neutral (e.g., because it can diversify its productive risk). Then

$$\frac{1}{U'(w_1 - Rl_1)} = \frac{1}{U'(w_2 - Rl_2)}$$

or, if the employee is risk-averse:

$$w_1 - Rl_1 = w_2 - Rl_2$$

Thus the utility level reached by the employee does not depend on the state of the world: He is fully insured by the firm. In this limited sense the model does justify the limited variation of wages during the cycle. On the other hand, it brings no new light on the variations of employment, since employment levels coincide with Walrasian ones in each state of the world.

The Asymmetric Information Optimum

Now assume that the firm learns the value of s at the beginning of the second period, before production takes place. On the other hand, the employee never learns the value of s. I will continue to assume that information is symmetric when the contract is signed; this therefore is a *hidden information* model, where information is symmetric ex ante and asymmetric ex post. The firm will of course be tempted to pretend that the price of the good is low so as to reduce the wage it pays to the employee; but the latter will anticipate such opportunistic behavior. The revelation principle introduced in chapter 2 again applies here: We can therefore concentrate attention on direct truthful contracts, that is, to four-tuples (l_1, w_1, l_2, w_2) such that the firm will find it best to reveal the true value of s once it observes it. The incentive constraints are

$$\begin{cases} s_1 g(l_1) - w_1 \geq s_1 g(l_2) - w_2 & (IC_1) \\ s_2 g(l_2) - w_2 \geq s_2 g(l_1) - w_1 & (IC_2) \end{cases}$$

and the optimal contract is obtained by minimizing the firm's objective

$$\pi_1 V(s_1 g(l_1) - w_1) + \pi_2 V(s_2 g(l_2) - w_2)$$

under the two incentive constraints (IC_1) and (IC_2) and the participation constraint (IR).

One can show that at the optimum, employment still is efficient when the price of the good is high, $l_2 = l_2^*$ or

$$s_2 g'(l_2) = R$$

but also that if the firm is risk-averse and the employee is almost risk-neutral, then there will be unemployment when the price of the good is low,

$$s_1 g'(l_1) > R$$

which implies $l_1 < l_1^*$ by the strict concavity of g.

The proof of these properties is made difficult by the fact that both the firm's and the employee's objectives appear in expectation in the maximization program, so the tools presented in chapter 2 do not directly apply. However, it is very easy to show a somewhat weaker result by transforming the program into the format of that studied in section 2.2. To do this, first note that looking for the optimal contract just amounts to looking for Pareto optima constrained by the incentive constraints. Thus we can turn the program upside down and maximize the employee's objective under the revelation constraints and a participation constraint for the firm:

$$\pi_1 V(s_1 g(l_1) - w_1) + \pi_2 V(s_2 g(l_2) - w_2) \geq \overline{V}$$

Now assume that the firm is infinitely risk-averse; its participation constraint then becomes

$$\min (s_1 g(l_1) - w_1, s_2 g(l_2) - w_2) \geq \overline{V}$$

which engenders the two constraints

$$\begin{cases} s_1 g(l_1) - w_1 \geq \overline{V} \\ s_2 g(l_2) - w_2 \geq \overline{V} \end{cases}$$

The reader will easily convince himself that the search for the maximum expected utility of the employee under both incentive constraints and both participation constraints is formally analogous to the program studied in section 2.2. The conclusions of our study of the latter program thus can be transposed directly. In particular, we already know that employment will be efficient in the favorable state and subefficient in the unfavorable state, which is precisely the conclusion we were after.

Note finally that the subefficiency of employment in the bad state is defined by a strict inequality $(s_1 g'(l_1) > R)$. Thus a continuity argument shows that the conclusion is still valid if the firm's risk-aversion is high enough.

Conclusion

The results presented above call for several remarks. First, it is not very satisfactory to invoke the firm's risk-neutrality to justify wage rigidity and its risk-aversion to justify unemployment at the trough of the business cycle. Moreover the unemployment result is sensitive to the specification of the employee's utility function, which we took to be $U(w - Rl)$. It can be proved that the result extends to the case where the employee has a more general utility function $U(w, l)$ only if leisure is an inferior good, which is not a very realistic assumption.[12]

Note also that the optimal contract is revealing, since $l_1 \neq l_2$. The employee thus knows the value taken by s when the firm proposes employment l. As we will see in chapter 6, the two parties then will find it mutually advantageous to renegotiate so as to avoid the inefficiency caused by unemployment when the state of the world is unfavorable. This is particularly important when the interaction is repeated and if the contract can be modified without waiting for the state of the world to change (see Dewatripont 1989); then renegotiation makes information revelation more progressive and reduces welfare.

Finally, we must come back to the nature of the contracts, which we have in fact treated as if they were explicit. In real life there are very few such explicit contracts. If they really are implicit contracts, then there must be a mechanism that ensures that they will be respected. Reputation effects are a natural candidate, since they imply that the firm may find it best in the long run to respect norms that may not be profitable in the short run. McLeod-Malcolmson

---

12. However, Hart (1983) shows that the unemployment result is robust if the employee has access to an insurance company.

(1989) study this question in a moral hazard model somewhat different from that I have presented.

The greatest failure of the theory of implicit contracts, apart from its special assumptions, is probably empirical: It predicts patterns of variation of unemployment among groups (countries, sectors, occupations) that we do not find in the data. Other competing theories fare much better on that score. This is the main reason why the theory of implicit contracts was all but abandoned in the 1980s.

3.2 Extensions

We will briefly study in this section a few of the main extensions of the theory developed in chapter 2. These cover competition among Principals or among Agents, risk-averse Agents, taking into account multidimensional characteristics, robust contracts, the introduction of asymmetric information on both sides, and countervailing incentives. This is not a representative summary of the literature: It reflects my personal biases. Still it should give the reader an idea of recent advances.

3.2.1 Competition in Contracts

Let us go back to the discrete model of section 2.2. How much profit π_i does the seller make on each type i of consumer? First note that he makes a positive profit on type 1, since

$$\pi_1 = \theta_1 q_1 - C(q_1) = \int_0^{q_1} (\theta_1 - C'(q))dq$$

and $C'(q) < C'(q_1) < \theta_1$ on $[0, q_1]$. Next consider the difference $\pi_2 - \pi_1$, and write it as

$$\pi_2 - \pi_1 = (\theta_2 - \theta_1)q_2 + \int_{q_1}^{q_2} (\theta_2 - C'(q))dq$$

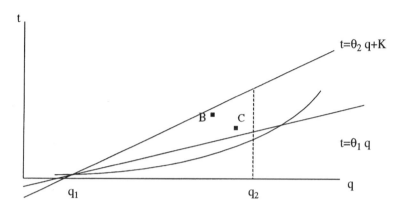

Figure 3.3
Competitive entry

Again $C'(q) \leq \theta_2$ on $[0, q_2]$, so both terms are positive. Thus the seller makes even more profit on type 2 Agents,[13] and this makes them more attractive to potential entrants in the wine market. If the Principal's monopoly power were to disappear, an entrant could propose the contract located in B on figure 3.3, capture the sophisticated consumers while leaving the coarse consumers to the Principal, and make positive profits.

Since the Principal loses a good share of his profits in the event, he is unlikely to stay inert. He can indeed react by offering, for instance, to the sophisticated consumers the contract C, which only leaves to the entrant the coarse consumers, and this is not the end of the story. What could be the competitive equilibria?[14]

To define a competitive equilibrium, we have to reach some notion of what makes a competitive configuration stable. This amounts to a game-theoretic description of actions and reactions when an entrant proposes a new contract. Assuming we have such a description, we

13. Again I have proved these results analytically, but they also obtain easily by looking at the figures.
14. I will only analyze here the free entry equilibria; Champsaur-Rochet (1989) study the duopoly case. Another important hidden assumption of my presentation is that an Agent cannot split his demand between competing Principals.

can then say that a *competitive equilibrium* is a set of profitable contracts (q, t) such that there is no other contract that can become a "profitable entrant." The Rothschild-Stiglitz equilibrium is the most popular concept of a competitive equilibrium.

The Rothschild-Stiglitz Equilibrium

The equilibrium concept proposed by Rothschild-Stiglitz (1976) in the context of insurance markets applies more generally to all adverse selection models. We will call a "profitable entrant" a contract that does not make losses if the other existing contracts are left unmodified. A Rothschild-Stiglitz equilibrium is such a set of contracts, of which none makes losses and such that no additional contract can be proposed that makes profits when the original contracts are left unmodified. In this particular sense it is a Nash equilibrium in a game among Principals where the strategies of the players are contracts.

First note that the number of contracts offered in equilibrium will clearly be no larger than the number of types, two here. If there is only one contract, it will be a *pooling* equilibrium; otherwise, it is a *separating* equilibrium.

Rothschild-Stiglitz started from the model discussed in section 3.1.3 and introduced competition. They showed that

• There exists no pooling equilibrium.

• There can exist only one separating equilibrium, which gives complete insurance to the high risks.

• This separating configuration may not be an equilibrium if the high-risk insurance buyers are relatively few in number.

Their most striking conclusion therefore was that there may exist no competitive equilibrium in insurance markets. However, and as I have already noted in section 3.1.3, the insurance model differs from the standard adverse selection model in several ways. Thus it is

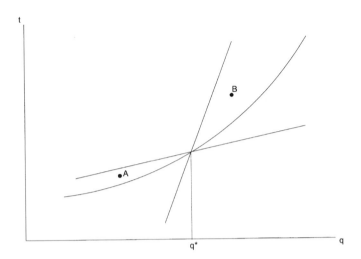

Figure 3.4
A candidate pooling equilibrium

interesting to examine the properties of the Rothschild-Stiglitz equilibrium (if it exists) within the standard model.

A graph will easily show us that there cannot exist a pooling equilibrium (q^*, t^*). It is indeed always possible to find (dq^*, dt^*) such that
the contract $(q^* + dq^*, t^* + dt^*)$ can be introduced and will make a
profit. Assume, for instance, that as in figure 3.4,

$$\theta_1 < C'(q^*) < \theta_2$$

In this situation an entrant can propose a contract in A and attract
the Agent of type 1, or alternatively propose a contract in B and
attract the Agent of type 2. Both types of contract make more profit
than (q^*, t^*), and they are therefore profitable entrants. The other
configurations can be analyzed on the same lines.

On the other hand, there is always a separating equilibrium; it is
the pair of contracts $((q_1, t_1), (q_2, t_2))$ such that

$$\begin{cases} C'(q_1) = \theta_1 \\ C'(q_2) = \theta_2 \\ \quad t_1 = C(q_1) \\ \quad t_2 = C(q_2) \end{cases}$$

This case is illustrated in figure 3.5.

This type of contract obviously is an equilibrium, since any other contract preferred by a consumer must make losses. Moreover it is Pareto optimal, since it gives to each type of consumer his efficient quality. However, note that transfers are much lower here than at the industry optimum in the monopoly problem: Each consumer has a positive surplus, and the Principal gets zero profits, contrary to the monopoly situation where the Principal makes profits and the Agents have zero surplus.

It is easy to check that there cannot be any other equilibrium. Indeed, every equilibrium must be efficient; otherwise, an entrant could propose a contract that increases the Agent's utility and makes positive profits. Moreover the equilibrium we just characterized obviously is the only efficient equilibrium.

These results strikingly differ from those Rothschild and Stiglitz obtained by applying their equilibrium concept to insurance markets. It turns out that the crucial modeling difference is that in the insurance model the Agent's type figures prominently in the Principal's utility function.

The Rothschild-Stiglitz equilibrium concept has been widely criticized, mainly because it assumes that incumbent firms stay inert

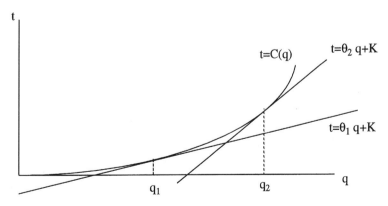

Figure 3.5
The competitive equilibrium

when an entrant arrives. Other equilibrium concepts have been proposed to restore the existence of an equilibrium in competitive insurance markets. They differ according to how they assume incumbent vendors react to entry (by withdrawing contracts that start making losses, by proposing new contracts, etc.) and how they describe the entrant's behavior. In our standard model a contract makes profits or losses independently of the type of the Agent who buys it;[15] therefore the configuration exhibited above still will be a competitive equilibrium, no matter how we change (within reason) the equilibrium concept.

To conclude, let me point out that there are at least two other ways to model competition between (a small number of) Principals. The first one is analyzed in the paper by Champsaur-Rochet (1989), who consider the case of a duopoly. Champsaur and Rochet start from the vertical differentiation model with continuous types studied by Mussa-Rosen (1978). In that model a monopoly chooses to offer a range of qualities to the various types of buyers. Champsaur and Rochet show that when two firms compete in prices and qualities, it is optimal for them to offer two disjoint ranges of qualities, so that one of the firms specializes in higher qualities and the other specializes in lower qualities. It is also possible to model an Agent who faces two Principals, each of whom offers a direct truthful mechanism. The Agent chooses his announcements so as to maximize his utility, while the two Principals play a Nash equilibrium: Each chooses the best contract given the choice of the other Principal. This model is called a *common agency* model, or a *multiprincipals* model. The conclusions of this model strongly differ according to whether the two activities regulated by the two Principals are complements or substitutes in the Agent's utility function. Take, for instance, the case where the Agent is a firm and the two Principals, respectively, control its production and its pollution level; then the two activities

---

15. The situation clearly is quite different in insurance markets, since there a contract may make profits when it is bought by low risks and losses when it is bought by high risks.

are complements and the noncooperative behavior of the Principals tends to both increase distortions and reduce the Agent's rent. In the polar case when the two activities are substitutes, for instance, because the Agent is a multinational and the Principals are two governments that tax its production in two different countries, then the noncooperative behavior of the Principals both reduces distortions and increases the Agent's rent. See Martimort (1992) and Stole (1990) for the general theory and Martimort (1996) for an example.

3.2.2   The Theory of Auctions

The previous subsection covered competition between Principals. The theory of auctions belongs to the dual topic of competition between Agents. I will not try to cover here such a vast field;[16] I will only present one of the simplest models of auctions.

Auctions are traditionally classified into two groups: *independent private values auctions* and *common value auctions*. The sale of a durable good such as a painting or a house is the typical example of an independent private values auction: The value of the good for each potential buyer is known only to himself, and these values are statistically independent. The situation is quite different in a common values auction: The value of the good then is the same for each potential buyer, but neither the buyer nor the seller fully knows this value; each buyer only observes a signal of his reservation value. The sale of the rights to drill in an oil tract is the most often quoted example. Note that these two types of auctions can actually be studied together inside a more general setup (Milgrom-Weber 1982).

Auctions are one of the most anciently used economic mechanisms. They are still intensively used, for traditional purposes such as the selling of timber but also for pricing Treasury bonds in the United States or for selecting firms to operate public utilities. A

---

16. The reader could consult the light introduction by Milgrom (1989) or the more complete survey by McAfee-McMillan (1987).

recent multibillion dollar example is the auction for spectrum licenses organized by the Federal Communications Commission, which started in 1994.

The most usual mechanisms are[17]

· the ascending auction (*English auction*), where bidders raise the price until only one of them remains;

· the descending auction (*Dutch auction*), where an auctioneer quotes decreasing prices until a bidder claims the good;

· two types of auctions where bidders submit sealed bids and the winner is the bidder who quoted the highest bid: In the *first-price sealed bid auction* the winner pays the sum he quoted, and in the *second-price sealed bid auction* the winner pays the value of the second-highest bid.

I will only study here the first-price sealed bid, independent private values auction. Let there be n potential buyers whose valuation of the good is drawn from a continuous distribution of probability distribution function f and of cumulative distribution function F on $[\underline{\theta}, \bar{\theta}]$. I will denote by $(\theta_1, \ldots, \theta_n)$ the valuations of the n buyers and by $(\theta_{(1)}, \ldots, \theta_{(n)})$ the corresponding *order statistics*: $\theta_{(1)}$ is the highest of all θ_i, $\theta_{(2)}$ the second-highest, and so on.

I will focus on symmetric equilibria with increasing bids. It can be shown that there exists no other equilibrium (in this very simple setting) if the buyers' bids are bounded below, for example, by 0. Thus assume that the buyers $2, \ldots, n$ submit bids $(b_2, \ldots, b_n)$ that are linked to their respective valuations through an increasing function B so that $b_i = B(\theta_i)$. Then buyer 1 will win the auctioned good if and only if he submits a higher bid, namely, if and only if

$$\forall i = 2, \ldots, n, \quad b_1 \geq B(\theta_i)$$

which happens with probability

17. There are many other, more or less exotic auctions; for example, see Riley-Samuelson (1981).

$$\Pr\left(\forall\, i = 2, \dots, n\,,\, \theta_i \le B^{-1}(b_1)\right) = F\left(B^{-1}(b_1)\right)^{n-1}$$

Buyer 1 then gets a surplus $(\theta_1 - b_1)$. I will assume that buyers are risk-neutral; then the expected utility of buyer 1 is

$$(\theta_1 - b_1)F\left(B^{-1}(b_1)\right)^{n-1}$$

Buyer 1 must maximize this expression in b_1. Let $\pi_1(\theta_1)$ denote the value of the optimum:

$$\pi_1(\theta_1) = \max_{b_1}\left((\theta_1 - b_1)F\left(B^{-1}(b_1)\right)^{n-1}\right)$$

By the envelope theorem, we get

$$\frac{d\pi_1}{d\theta_1}(\theta_1) = F\left(B^{-1}(b_1)\right)^{n-1}$$

Our interest lies in symmetric Nash equilibria, in which all bidders adopt the same increasing strategy B; therefore we must have $b_1 = B(\theta_1)$, whence

$$\frac{d\pi_1}{d\theta_1}(\theta_1) = F(\theta_1)^{n-1} \qquad (D)$$

The expected utility of a buyer with the lowest possible valuation must be zero:[18] $\pi_1(\underline{\theta}) = 0$. Therefore, by integrating the differential equation (D),

$$\pi_1(\theta_1) = \int_{\underline{\theta}}^{\theta_1} F(\theta)^{n-1} d\theta$$

Note that $\pi_1(\theta_1)$ is the informational rent of the buyer of valuation θ_1. Thus we find again a property we already obtained in the previous chapter: The informational rent of the buyer with the lowest possible valuation $\underline{\theta}$ is zero, and that of the other buyers is positive and increases with their type.

---

18. Since the function B is increasing, this buyer indeed wins the auction with zero probability.

Since

$$\pi_1(\theta_1) = (\theta_1 - B(\theta_1))F(\theta_1)^{n-1}$$

we finally get the equilibrium strategy

$$B(\theta_1) = \theta_1 - \frac{\int_{\underline{\theta}}^{\theta_1} F(\theta)^{n-1}d\theta}{F(\theta_1)^{n-1}}$$

which indeed is an increasing function, as assumed earlier. Note that this implies that the equilibrium is revealing.

In equilibrium, bidders therefore submit a bid that is lower than their valuation for the good: They *shade* their bid. In order to win, it is indeed sufficient to submit a bid that is just higher than the second-highest bid; therefore the best strategy is to estimate the latter and to try to just overbid it. We can confirm this intuition by integrating by parts

$$\int_{\underline{\theta}}^{\theta_1} F(\theta)^{n-1}d\theta = \theta_1 F(\theta_1)^{n-1} - \int_{\underline{\theta}}^{\theta_1} (n-1)\theta F(\theta)^{n-2}f(\theta)d\theta$$

so that we can rewrite the function B as

$$B(\theta_1) = \frac{\int_{\underline{\theta}}^{\theta_1} (n-1)\theta F(\theta)^{n-2}f(\theta)d\theta}{F(\theta_1)^{n-1}}$$

It is easy to check that $(n-1)F(\theta)^{n-2}f(\theta)/F(\theta_1)^{n-1}$ is the probability distribution function of the conditional distribution of $\theta_{(2)}$ given that $\theta_{(1)} = \theta_1$. We finally have

$$B(\theta_1) = E(\theta_{(2)} | \theta_{(1)} = \theta_1)$$

which shows that every potential buyer computes his bid by assuming he will win and estimating the value of the second-highest valuation.

Note that if we adopt the seller's point of view, namely, if we integrate once more, we get the expectation of the winning bid

$$EB(\theta_{(1)}) = E\theta_{(2)}$$

This equality suggests two remarks. First, it is clear that $\theta_{(2)}$ is an increasing function of the number of potential buyers n: The more numerous the bidders are, the more their valuations will be spread. As $EB(\theta_{(1)})$ is the seller's expected revenue, we can conclude that the competition between buyers embodied in the auction mechanism allows the seller to extract an expected revenue that increases with the number of bidders. If that number goes to infinity, $\theta_{(2)}$ converges to the highest possible valuation $\bar{\theta}$ and in the limit, the seller appropriates all the surplus.

Second, the equation that gives the seller's expected revenue happens to hold in all of the four independent private values auction mechanisms I listed earlier: If (as we assumed) agents are risk-neutral, then the seller's expected revenue does not depend on the auction mechanism he uses. This property, whose first proof is due to Vickrey (1961), is often called the *revenue equivalence theorem*. It implies that the reasons why a seller decides to choose a particular auction must be looked for in a more general model than that presented here. Introducing risk-averse buyers or the possibility of collusive strategies, for instance, breaks the revenue equivalence theorem.

Even within our symmetric, independent private values setting, the choice of the optimal auction has generated some interest. There are two viewpoints for studying the optimality of an auction. First, we may want to design a socially efficient auction, one that maximizes social surplus. Since the latter is just $(\theta_i - \theta_0)$ when the seller's valuation for the good is θ_0 and he sells to buyer i, a socially efficient auction is just one that sells the good to the buyer with the highest valuation.[19] Thus the first-price sealed-bid auction is socially efficient. Second, the seller himself is interested in designing the auction that will give him the highest expected utility. The literature has focused on this more difficult topic, and from now on "optimal" will mean "optimal for the seller." It turns out that the optimal auction is

---

19. We can assume that the good will be sold anyway.

socially efficient when buyers are symmetric (i.e., their valuations are drawn from the same probability distribution); however, this is not true anymore when buyers are asymmetric.[20]

Finding the optimal auction is equivalent to finding the optimal direct truthful mechanism $(x_i(\theta), t_i(\theta))_{i=1,\ldots,n}$, where x_i is the probability that buyer i gets the good, t_i is his expected payment, and θ is the n-uple of valuations. Let us first focus, as in Riley-Samuelson (1981), on the more restricted question of the optimal reserve price the seller should fix in the first-price sealed-bid auction.

Assume therefore that before the auction starts, the seller announces that he will not award the good if all bids are lower than some reserve price b_r. It is easy to see, going through the characterization of the equilibrium bids above, that they are now given by

$$B(\theta_1) = \theta_1 - \frac{\int_{b_r}^{\theta_1} F(\theta)^{n-1} d\theta}{F(\theta_1)^{n-1}}$$

for $\theta_1 \geq b_r$ (they are undetermined for $\theta_1 < b_r$). Since $B(b_r) = b_r$, this implies that the good will be sold only if the highest valuation exceeds b_r. Now let θ_0 be the seller's valuation for the good. Exercise 3.4 asks you to show that the optimal reserve price is given by

$$b_r - \frac{1 - F(b_r)}{f(b_r)} = \theta_0$$

The left-hand side of this equation is called the *virtual valuation* associated with the valuation b_r. If the hazard rate of F is nondecreasing, then the virtual valuation increases with the valuation, and there is a unique solution b_r. Note that the optimal b_r is larger than the seller's valuation, so there may be unrealized gains from trade: cases

20. The reason is that the optimal auction takes into account the virtual valuations of buyers, which depend on the hazard rates of the probability distributions. With asymmetric buyers it is easy to see that comparing virtual valuations is not equivalent to comparing valuations.

in which the highest valuation of the buyers is larger than θ_0, and yet smaller than b_r, so that the good is not sold.

Now let us come back to our original question. What is the optimal auction if it can take any form? Myerson (1981) shows that the answer is strikingly simple: The auction characterized above with its optimally set reserve price is optimal. Thus there is no gain for the seller in using very complicated auction mechanisms. Myerson's paper is technically demanding, but Bulow-Roberts (1989) gives a much simpler introduction to this literature.

3.2.3   Risk-Averse Agents

We have assumed so far that the contract between the Principal and the Agent was signed after the Agent learned his private information. In some situations it may be more realistic to assume that the Agent learns his private information after the contract is signed but before it is executed. Consider, for instance, a chain monopoly in which the unknown variable is the strength of demand. Before the sales campaign starts, manufacturer and retailer sign a contract that specifies a nonlinear tariff to be used between them. After the contract is signed, the retailer gradually learns the strength of demand; however, the manufacturer can only acquire information by observing the orders the retailer places with him. The Agent here still has an informational advantage, but that comes from knowing he will soon be better informed than the Principal. As already mentioned in section 3.1.4, this is sometimes called a *hidden information* model.

Salanié (1990) studies just such a model. The formal difference with the standard model here is that since the Agent does not know his characteristic when the contract is signed, his participation constraint should be written in an expected utility form:

$$\int_{\underline{\theta}}^{\overline{\theta}} U\Big(u(q(\theta), \theta) - t(\theta)\Big) f(\theta) d\theta \geq U(0)$$

where U is the Agent's von Neumann-Morgenstern utility function.

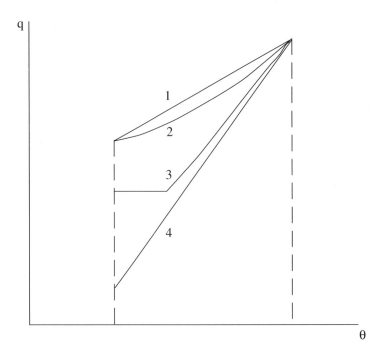

Figure 3.6
The optimal allocation with a risk-averse agent: (1) $\sigma = 0$; (2) σ small; (3) σ large;
(4) σ infinite

This makes solving the model much more difficult[21] but also gives
the solution interesting properties. Figure 3.6 gives the shape of the
optimal allocation $q(\theta)$ as a function of the strength of demand θ for
several values of the Agent's absolute risk-aversion index σ.

For any given θ, the optimal allocation is a decreasing function of
the risk-aversion parameter. The interesting feature of the solution is
that it involves bunching for a large but finite risk-aversion. This is
in contrast with the two polar cases of zero or infinite risk-aversion,
in which the optimal allocation fully separates types. The standard
model is obtained by letting σ be infinite; indeed, the participation
constraint then is

---

21. The Pontryagin minimum principle should be used here, and it yields (even in
the simplest specification) a nonlinear second-order differential equation in q with
fixed ends.

$\forall \theta, \quad u(q(\theta), \theta) - t(\theta) \geq 0$

as in chapter 2. Thus focusing on the standard model, in which bunching can be excluded with a monotone hazard rate condition, may induce us to underestimate the extent of bunching.

3.2.4 Multidimensional Characteristics

So far we have focused on the case where the Agent's private characteristic is one-dimensional. Clearly it is important to check that the results obtained in that case extend to settings in which θ is multidimensional. Unfortunately, the study of this extension is fairly involved. The analysis started with Laffont-Maskin-Rochet (1985), who showed that the optimum was much more likely to display bunching than in the one-dimensional case. Two recent papers have obtained sharper results. Armstrong (1996) shows that for all specifications, some Agents are excluded at the optimum. This is in contrast with the one-dimensional case in which it is always possible to find conditions such that all Agents participate at the optimum. The intuition is fairly simple: If the Principal increases his tariff uniformly by a small ε, he will increase his profits by a term of order ε on all Agents who still participate, but he will lose all Agents whose surplus was smaller than ε. However, when θ is multidimensional, the probability that an Agent has surplus lower than ε is a higher-order term in ε. Thus it pays to slightly increase the tariff, even if the Principal thereby excludes some Agents.

The paper by Rochet-Choné (1997) studies the two-dimensional problem. He reaches several distressing conclusions:

• When the correlation between the one-dimensional components of the characteristic is strongly negative, upward or transverse incentive constraints may be binding at the optimum.

• The solution may be stochastic.

• Most strikingly, bunching appears to be a generic property in multidimensional problems; no simple condition on the primitives of

the problem (e.g., a multidimensional generalization of the monotone hazard rate condition) can exclude it.

Thus the nice properties obtained in the one-dimensional case do
not appear to carry over to multidimensional problems. This is
clearly a challenge for the theory.

3.2.5   Robustness and Observation Errors

In practice, the optimal mechanism $(q(\theta), t(\theta))$ is generally used
through the nonlinear tariff $t = \tau(q)$ that is associated to it by the taxation principle. If q can only be observed with an error, it is not clear
that the contract will still be optimal.

Assume that the Principal can only observe $Q = q + \varepsilon$, where ε is
an observational noise whose distribution is known and that the
Agent cannot control. If the tariff τ is not linear, then using it will
lead the Agent to choose levels of q that solve

$$\max_q \left(u(q, \theta) - E\tau(q + \varepsilon)\right)$$

and these generally differ from the optimal $q(\theta)$: Only linear contracts are robust to the introduction of noise.

In these circumstances one should use more general mechanisms
that allow for what is usually called "preplay communication." The
optimal mechanism a priori is a menu of tariffs $t = \tau_\theta(Q)$: If the
Agent announces θ, the Principal asks him to choose a q and makes
him pay $\tau_\theta(Q)$. The Agent must therefore solve

$$\max_{\hat{\theta}, q} \left(u(q, \theta) - E\tau_{\hat{\theta}}(q + \varepsilon)\right)$$

Under some conditions there will exist a function $\hat{\tau}$ such that

$$\forall q, \tau(q) = E\hat{\tau}(q + \varepsilon)$$

The Principal can then replace the tariff $\tau(q)$ with the tariff $\hat{\tau}(Q)$ and
implement the same allocation (Caillaud-Guesnerie-Rey 1992). This

solution of the problem of observational errors assumes of course that the Principal has a full knowledge of the characteristics of the noise ε. Moreover it relies strongly on the Agent's utility function being quasi-linear: If the Agent were to be risk-averse with respect to income, then it would be necessary to use the full flexibility of the family of tariffs $\tau_\theta(Q)$; preplay communication (through the announcement of θ) then becomes valuable (see Melumad-Reichelstein 1989).

3.2.6 Bilateral Private Information

Some economists take the theory of contracts to task because much of it focuses on models in which only one party possesses private information. They argue that in the real world, private information tends to be widely dispersed through the economy; in most two-party relationships both parties have their share of private information. This suggests that we should study models in which the private information is distributed more symmetrically than it is in the models of chapter 2. The next paragraphs describe two such models. We will first describe a mechanism design problem between a seller and a buyer, both of which have private information on their own valuation. Then we will study an extension of the Principal-Agent adverse selection model in which the Principal too has some private information.

The Inefficiency of Trading Mechanisms

Myerson-Satterthwaite (1983) consider a transaction on a 0–1 good between a seller of valuation c and a buyer of valuation v. Efficiency then requires that trading occur if and only if v is greater than c. Only the seller knows c and only the buyer knows v. The valuations c and v are independently distributed with respective probability distribution functions f_1 on $[\underline{c}, \overline{c}]$ and f_2 on $[\underline{v}, \overline{v}]$, both of which are positive on their whole domains. Our problem is to find an efficient trading mechanism that is incentive compatible and individually rational.

Thus we look for two functions $x(c, v)$ (the probability of trading the good) and $t(c, v)$ (the transfer from the buyer to the seller)

- that are efficient: $x(c, v) = 1$ if $v \geq c$, $x(c, v) = 0$ otherwise;
- that are incentive compatible for both the seller, c maximizes

$$\int_{\underline{v}}^{\bar{v}} \left(t(c', v) - cx(c', v) \right) f_2(v) dv \quad \text{over } c'$$

and the buyer, v maximizes

$$\int_{\underline{c}}^{\bar{c}} \left(vx(c, v') - t(c, v') \right) f_1(c) dc \quad \text{over } v'$$

- that are individually rational for both the seller,

$$\forall c, \quad \int_{\underline{v}}^{\bar{v}} \left(t(c, v) - cx(c, v) \right) f_2(v) dv \geq 0$$

and the buyer:

$$\forall v, \quad \int_{\underline{c}}^{\bar{c}} \left(vx(c, v) - t(c, v) \right) f_1(c) dc \geq 0$$

These formulas may look impressive, but they are just the same as in chapter 2, with the only difference that since each party ignores the characteristic of the other party, he must compute his expected utility by integrating over it.

Let us first deal with two trivial cases. First, if $\bar{v} < \underline{c}$, it is common knowledge that there are no gains from trade. Then $x(c, v) = t(c, v) = 0$ solves our problem. Things are almost as simple if it is common knowledge that there are gains from trade: $\bar{c} < \underline{v}$. Then any mechanism that prescribes $x(c, v) = 1$ and $t(c, v) = T$, with $\bar{c} \leq T \leq \underline{v}$, is efficient, incentive compatible, and individually rational.

The interesting case comes when there is a positive probability of gains from trade ($\underline{c} < \bar{v}$) but also a positive probability of no gains from trade ($\underline{v} < \bar{c}$). Then Myerson-Satterthwaite show that there exists no efficient trading mechanism that is both incentive compatible and individually rational.

Note that we have assumed nothing whatsoever on how the trading mechanism is to be chosen (through the Principal-Agent paradigm, some form of bargaining between buyer and seller, a rule imposed by a third party, etc.) Thus this is a very strong inefficiency result that goes against the grain of "results" such as the celebrated Coase theorem, whose optimistic version asserts that in the absence of transaction costs, agents may always bargain away any inefficiency.

The Informed Principal

Let us now come back within the more specific Principal-Agent model. In real-life situations the Principal often has himself some private information. This may directly concern the Agent (in which case we speak of *common values*) or not (then we speak of *private values*).[22] We will only study here the case where values are private; the reader can consult Maskin-Tirole (1992) for the analysis of the common values case, which we will also come back to in chapter 4.

Let us come back again to the standard model with a discriminating wine seller; if the seller's production cost depends on a parameter λ which he is the only one to observe, then we are in an informed Principal private values model, since λ does not figure in the Agent's utility function. Let us denote utility functions as

$$V(q, t, \lambda)$$

for the Principal and

$$U(q, t, \theta)$$

for the Agent. Each of the two parties now has its own private information. A direct truthful mechanism here is a menu of contracts (q, t) indexed by both parameters θ and λ such that when both parties

---

22. This terminology clearly has no relationship to that we use in the theory of auctions.

announce their characteristic simultaneously, truthtelling is their best strategy. Let $(q(\theta; \lambda), t(\theta; \lambda))$ be the menu of contracts that is optimal in the uninformed Principal model when λ is public information; the type λ Principal can always propose this menu of contracts when his private information is λ and thus guarantee himself the same utility as when λ is public information. Maskin-Tirole (1990) in fact show that for a generic subset of utility functions,[23] the Principal can actually do better and obtain a higher utility than if he were to reveal his information before proposing the contract. To see why, let P be the probability distribution of the different types of Principal for the Agent; since the Agent does not know the type of the Principal when the contract is signed and only learns it after θ and λ are simultaneously revealed, the incentive and individual rationality constraints of the Agent in the Principal's program must be written as expectations over P. On the other hand, if λ was public information, these constraints would have to hold for all values of λ. Therefore the Principal's program is less constrained when he only reveals his characteristic after the contract is signed. He thus gets a higher utility thanks to his private information, even though the Agent does not particularly care about the Principal's characteristic. Note, however, that in the particular case of quasi-linear utilities on which we mostly focused attention, it is easy to show that the Principal gains nothing by withholding his private information. Thus the private values case with quasi-linear utilities does not appear to modify the properties of the optimum in adverse selection models.

3.2.7   Countervailing Incentives

We have seen that in adverse selection models, informational rents are the price that the Principal must pay in order to induce the Agent to reveal his type. Take, for instance, the regulation of a public firm;

---

23. We say a property is "generic" when the subsets of objects to which it does not apply has measure zero, or (in infinite dimensions) when this subset is closed with an empty interior.

only the firm observes its marginal cost, and it will naturally want to pretend its costs are higher than they actually are so as to be allowed to set a higher price. The rule that price should equal marginal cost therefore cannot be applied when the regulator does not know the costs of the firm. In fact the price must be set above marginal cost for all but the most efficient firms. This clearly involves inefficiencies.

It may be, however, that special features of the models counteract this inefficiency. Assume, for instance, that the firm's fixed costs are inversely correlated to its marginal cost: When the latter is c, fixed costs are $F(c)$, where F is a known concave[24] decreasing function. Then the firm faces *countervailing incentives*: it would like to quote a high c so as to set a high price, but at the same time it is tempted to underquote c so that its fixed costs are refunded more generously. Lewis-Sappington (1989) show that when c is low enough, the usual argument is valid and the price will be above marginal cost. On the other hand, when c is high (and fixed costs are low), the Principal will actually set the price *below* marginal cost. Moreover there will be bunching (price will be independent of costs) in an intermediate range of c.

Beyond the specific features of the solution, the general lesson to remember here is that if countervailing incentives exist, they will tend to reduce the inefficiencies involved in adverse selection models. Thus the Principal should try to create countervailing incentives if he can.

Exercises

Exercise 3.1

Going back to the optimal taxation model of section 3.1.2, let $T(\theta) = Q(\theta) - C(\theta)$ be the tax paid by Agent θ. Assume that the optimum is fully separating.

---

24. The concavity assumption is imposed for technical reasons.

1. Show that the marginal tax rate $T'(\theta)$ is given by

$T'(\theta) = (\theta U'(C(\theta)) - 1)C'(\theta)$

2. Show that $T'(\underline{\theta}) = T'(\bar{\theta}) = 0$ and that $T'(\theta) > 0$ everywhere else.

3. How does this compare with the tax schedules actually used in your country?

Exercise 3.2

Show directly that in the standard model, any Rothschild-Stiglitz equilibrium must be efficient (you should use figures).

Exercise 3.3

Wilson (1977) argued that in a competitive equilibrium an incumbent firm should be able to withdraw a contract that has become unprofitable because of a profitable entry. A Wilson competitive equilibrium therefore is a set of profitable contracts such that no entrant can propose a contract that remains profitable after all unprofitable contracts are withdrawn. It can be shown that a Wilson equilibrium always exists in the competitive insurance model, and that it coincides with the Rothschild-Stiglitz equilibrium when the latter exists.

Show that the Wilson equilibrium coincides with the Rothschild-Stiglitz equilibrium in the standard model.

Exercise 3.4

In this exercise you will derive the optimal reserve price in the simple auction of section 3.2.2. You may admit the formula for the equilibrium bid as a function of b_r.

1. Let $P(\theta_1)$ be the expected payment of agent 1 when $\theta_1 \geq b_r$. Show that

$$P(\theta_1) = \theta_1 F(\theta_1)^{n-1} - \int_{b_r}^{\theta_1} F(\theta)^{n-1} d\theta$$

2. Now let R be the expected revenue of the seller, which equals $n\int_{b_r}^{\bar{\theta}} P(\theta_1) f(\theta_1) d\theta_1$. Integrating by parts, show that

$$R = n\int_{b_r}^{\bar{\theta}} \left(\theta f(\theta) + F(\theta) - 1 \right) F^{n-1}(\theta) d\theta$$

3. Show that the seller's expected utility is $(\theta_0 F^n(b_r) + R)$, and differentiate with respect to b_r so as to obtain the formula given in 3.2.2.

References

Armstrong, M. 1996. Multiproduct nonlinear pricing. *Econometrica* 64:51–75.

Azariadis, C. 1975. Implicit contracts and underemployment equilibria. *Journal of Political Economy* 83:1183-1202.

Baron, D., and R. Myerson. 1982. Regulating a monopolist with unknown cost. *Econometrica* 50:911–30.

Bulow, J., and J. Roberts. 1989. The simple economics of optimal auctions. *Journal of Political Economy* 97:1060–90.

Caillaud, B., R. Guesnerie, and P. Rey. 1992. Noisy observation in adverse selection models. *Review of Economic Studies* 59:595–615.

Caillaud, B., R. Guesnerie, P. Rey, and J. Tirole. 1988. Government intervention in production and incentives theory: A review of recent contributions. *Rand Journal of Economics* 19:1–26.

Champsaur, P., and J.-C. Rochet. 1989. Multiproduct duopolists. *Econometrica* 57:533–57.

Dewatripont, M. 1989. Renegotiation and information revelation over time: The case of optimal labor contracts. *Quarterly Journal of Economics* 104:589–619.

Hart, O. 1983. Optimal labor contracts under asymmetric information: An introduction. *Review of Economic Studies* 50:3–35.

Laffont, J.-J. 1994. The new economics of regulation ten years after. *Econometrica* 62:507–37.

Laffont, J.-J., E. Maskin, and J.-C. Rochet. 1987. Optimal nonlinear pricing with two-dimensional characteristics. In *Information, Incentives and Economic Mechanisms: In*

Honor of L. Hurwicz, T. Groves, R. Radner, and S. Reiter, eds. Saint-Paul: University of Minnesota Press.

Laffont, J.-J., and J. Tirole. 1986. Using cost observation to regulate firms. *Journal of Political Economy* 94:614–41.

Laffont, J.-J., and J. Tirole. 1993. *A Theory of Incentives in Procurement and Regulation.* Cambridge: MIT Press.

Lewis, T., and D. Sappington. 1989. Countervailing incentives in agency problems. *Journal of Economic Theory* 49:294–313.

Lollivier, S., and J.-C. Rochet. 1983. Bunching and second-order conditions: A note on optimal tax theory. *Journal of Economic Theory* 31:392–400.

Martimort, D. 1992. Multi-principaux avec sélection adverse. *Annales d'Economie et de Statistique* 28:1–38.

Martimort, D. 1996. Exclusive dealing, common agency and multiprincipals incentive theory. *Rand Journal of Economics* 27:1–31.

Maskin, E., and J. Tirole. 1990. The Principal-Agent relationship with an informed Principal. I: Private values. *Econometrica* 58:379–409.

Maskin, E., and J. Tirole. 1992. The Principal-Agent relationship with an informed Principal. II: Common values. *Econometrica* 60:1–42.

McAfee, P., and J. McMillan. 1987. Auctions and bidding. *Journal of Economic Literature* 25:699–738.

McLeod, B., and J. Malcolmson. 1989. Implicit contracts, incentive compatibility and involuntary unemployment. *Econometrica* 57:447–80.

Melumad, N., and S. Reichelstein. 1989. The value of communication in agencies. *Journal of Economic Theory* 18:296–307.

Milgrom, P. 1989. Auctions and bidding: A primer. *Journal of Economic Perspectives* 3:3–22.

Milgrom, P., and R. Weber. 1982. A theory of auctions and competitive bidding. *Econometrica* 50:1089–1122.

Mirrlees, J. 1986. The theory of optimal taxation. In *Handbook of Mathematical Economics,* vol. 3, K. Arrow and M. Intriligator, eds. Amsterdam: North-Holland.

Mussa, M., and S. Rosen. 1978. Monopoly and product quality. *Journal of Economic Theory* 18:301–17.

Myerson, R. 1981. Optimal auction design. *Mathematics of Operation Research* 6:58–73.

Myerson, R., and M. Satterthwaite. 1983. Efficient mechanisms for bilateral trading. *Journal of Economic Theory* 28:265–81.

Riley, J., and W. Samuelson. 1981. Optimal auctions. *American Economic Review* 71:381–92.

Rochet, J.-C, and P. Choné. 1997. Ironing, sweeping and multidimensional screening. Forthcoming in *Econometrica*.

Rothschild, M., and J. Stiglitz. 1976. Equilibrium in competitive insurance markets. *Quarterly Journal of Economics* 90:629–49.

Salanié, B. 1990. Sélection adverse et aversion pour le risque. *Annales d'Economie et de Statistique* 18:131–49.

Stiglitz, J. 1977. Monopoly, nonlinear pricing, and imperfect information: The insurance market. *Review of Economic Studies* 44:407–30.

Stole, L. 1990. Mechanism design under common agency. Mimeo.

Vickrey, W. 1961. Counterspeculation, auctions, and competitive sealed tenders. *Journal of Finance* 16:8–37.

Wilson, C. 1977. A model of insurance markets with incomplete information. *Journal of Economic Theory* 16:167–207.

4   Signaling Models

In adverse selection models the uninformed party takes the initiative by offering to the informed party a menu of contracts between which the different types of informed agents choose according to their private characteristics. In real life it is sometimes difficult to determine whether the initiative resides with the informed party or with the uninformed party; the institutional context matters a great deal and varies considerably across specific situations. Most economic relationships moreover are repeated, which makes it difficult to observe the extensive form of the game. It is therefore important to also study games in which the informed party plays first by sending a signal that may reveal information relating to its type. The uninformed party then tries to decrypt these signals by using some (endogeneously determined) interpretative scheme.

We will study three types of models in this chapter. The first one is due to Akerlof (1970); it shows that a market may function very badly if the informed party has no way to signal the quality of the good it is selling. In the second model, due to Spence (1973), the signal that is sent by the informed party has a cost that depends on its type so that, roughly speaking, higher types are more likely to send higher signals. This signal may then help the uninformed party to distinguish the different types. We will analyze in a third part the Crawford-Sobel (1982) model which shows that even if the signal is purely extrinsic (if it has no cost for the informed party) and thus constitutes *cheap talk*, both parties may still coordinate on equilibria that reveal some information.

A typical feature of signaling models of the Spence and Crawford-Sobel type is that contrary to adverse selection models, they possess a large number of equilibria. While this multiplicity can be eliminated by using refinements of perfect Bayesian equilibrium in Spence's model, it is a robust feature of the Crawford-Sobel model.

Parts of this chapter use intuitions of game theory that are more advanced than in the rest of the book. The appendix to this book presents some equilibrium concepts for the readers who may not be familiar with them.

4.1 The Market for Second-hand Cars

In a classic paper Akerlof (1970) showed that uncertainty as to the quality of a good may hinder the functioning of the market. Suppose that two types of cars coexist on the market for second-hand cars: good cars and bad cars, so-called lemons in American slang. A good car is worth b to the seller and $B > b$ to the buyer, while a lemon is worth m to the seller and $M > m$ to the buyer. The proportion of good cars is q and that of lemons is $(1 - q)$. Note that since the value of any car to the buyer exceeds its value to the seller, with perfect information both types of cars should be traded.

We will assume that the supply of cars is finite but the number of potential buyers is infinite. Under these conditions the prices of good cars would settle in B and that of lemons in M if both sellers and buyers observe the quality of a given car. If both are equally ignorant of the quality of the cars, then the equilibrium price will be $(qB + (1 - q)M)$ whatever the car. In these two polar cases, all cars find a buyer.

It is of course easier for the seller than for the buyer to observe the quality of a car. We can therefore assume that the seller knows the quality of the cars he puts up for sale, while the buyer cannot observe this quality. What will be the equilibrium price p on the market?

First note that sellers will only offer good cars if the price p settles above b; otherwise they will lose money. If the price is lower than b, the buyers will know that all cars being offered are lemons; they will then buy if and only if the price is not above M. Now, if the price p is not below b, and both types of cars are put up for sale, then buyers will consider that a car is worth $(qB + (1 - q)M)$.

There are therefore only two possible equilibria:

- $p = M < b$ and only lemons are sold.
- $p = qB + (1 - q)M \geq b$ and both types of cars are sold.

The second equilibrium coincides with that of the model where neither buyer nor seller is informed of the quality, so there is no revelation of quality in equilibrium. But this can only be an equilibrium if $qB + (1 - q)M \geq b$; otherwise, the equilibrium must be the first one,[1] in which the lemons are chosen over good cars.

Informational asymmetries can thus hinder the functioning of the market where all types of cars are traded to the point where only low-quality goods are traded.[2] This is another striking example of adverse selection.

4.2   Costly Signals

The dysfunctioning of the market for second-hand cars analyzed by Akerlof comes from the inability of sellers of good cars to signal the quality of their good. If, for instance, they could publish the results of tests run on their cars by an independent laboratory, they would reduce the informational asymmetry that harms the buyers directly and themselves indirectly. I will not pursue this analogy here, but I will come back to Akerlof's model in section 4.4. I will now present Spence's model, which aims at describing how employers can infer the productivity of job searchers by checking their diplomas.

---

1. Since $qB + (1 - q)M < b$ implies that $M < b$, the first equilibrium exists.

2. In a model with continuous types of cars and for some parameter values, only the worst type of car may be traded, so the market essentially unravels. Mas Colell-Whinston-Green (1995, ch. 13) gives another example in the context of a labor market.

Each potential employee has a private information on his productivity $\theta \in \{\theta_1, \theta_2\}$, where $\theta_1 < \theta_2$; if he studies for e years and is hired at wage w, his utility will be $u(w) - C(e, \theta)$. His productivity does not depend on his education,[3] but getting a diploma costs him more when he is less productive:[4]

$$u' > 0, \quad u'' < 0;$$

$$\frac{\partial C}{\partial e} > 0, \quad \frac{\partial^2 C}{\partial e^2} > 0, \quad \frac{\partial^2 C}{\partial e \partial \theta} < 0$$

This last assumption on the cross-derivative can, for instance, be justified by the common notion that the ability to pursue higher studies and productivity are positively correlated, since they both depend on a common factor (e.g., general skills or readiness to work). It is important to emphasize that education may only serve as a signal here, since it does not enhance productivity.

The productivity of job searchers is their private information; however, diplomas are publicly observed.[5] The condition on the cross-derivative of C again is a Spence-Mirrlees condition; it plays the same role as in chapter 2, since it allows us to entertain the thought that employers could sort out job candidates by looking at their diplomas.

Potential employers are identical and compete à la Bertrand on the market for labor. Each worker is therefore paid his expected marginal productivity. A job searcher who enters the market with a diploma e thus will be offered a wage[6]

$$w(e) = \mu(e)\theta_1 + (1 - \mu(e))\theta_2$$

---

3. This is not essential here, but it makes the conclusions of the model more striking.
4. In all that follows, I will not distinguish between the number of years spent in school and the level of the most advanced diploma obtained.
5. We only need to assume that a job searcher who refuses to show his diploma will not be considered for hiring.
6. Strictly speaking, there is no contract in that model, but there is a system of norms (the link between diploma and wage) and an institution (Bertrand competition) that ensures that these norms is respected by employers.

if employers think that the candidate is θ_1 with probability $\mu(e)$. We will denote by μ_0 the a priori of employers on the worker's productivity.

This is a game of incomplete information in that, when taking their decisions, employers do not know the type of the worker. We will therefore look for the perfect Bayesian equilibria of this game.

Following the definition given in the appendix, a perfect Bayesian equilibrium in pure strategies consists of a vector of strategies (e_1^*, e_2^*, w^*) and a system of beliefs μ^* such that:

· Each job searcher chooses the number of years he will spend in school e by anticipating the wage function w^* that prevails on the labor market,

$$\forall i = 1, 2, \quad e_i^* \in \arg\max_e \left(u(w^*(e)) - C(e, \theta_i)\right)$$

· Each employer hires job searchers with a diploma e at a wage

$$w^*(e) = \mu^*(e)\theta_1 + (1 - \mu^*(e))\theta_2$$

· The beliefs $\mu^*(e)$ are consistent with the strategies e^*:

if $e_1^* \neq e_2^*$,

*if $e = e_1^*$: $\mu^*(e) = 1$

*if $e = e_2^*$: $\mu^*(e) = 0$

and if $e_1^* = e_2^*$,

*if $e = e_1^* = e_2^*$: $\mu^*(e) = \mu_0$

Note that this definition in no way restricts the beliefs $\mu^*(e)$ when diploma e is not chosen in equilibrium ($e \neq e_1^*$ and $e \neq e_2^*$). In that case we only know that the wage $w^*(e)$ must lie between θ_1 and θ_2. As we will see, the existence of this degree of freedom gives rise to a great multiplicity of perfect Bayesian equilibria; there will be both a continuum of separating equilibria and a continuum of pooling equilibria.[7]

---

7. I have focused on pure strategies equilibria here. Exercises 4.1 and 4.3 ask the reader to study semiseparating equilibria in which one of the two types randomizes between two education levels.

4.2.1   Separating Equilibria

In a separating equilibrium the low-productivity agent chooses to study for e_1^* years and the high-productivity agent studies for $e_2^* > e_1^*$ years. Employers can therefore infer the agent's productivity by looking at his diploma. The low-productivity agent gets a wage equal to θ_1, so his costly education is of no use to him. He therefore necessarily chooses not to study at all: $e_1^* = 0$. On the other hand, the high-productivity agent who studies for $e_2^* > 0$ years gets a wage θ_2. For this to be an equilibrium, the low-productivity agent must not envy the high-productivity agent his allocation; in other words, we must have

$$u(\theta_1) - C(0, \theta_1) \geq u(\theta_2) - C(e_2^*, \theta_1)$$

which tells us that e_2^* should not be below a certain $\underline{e}$. Symmetrically, θ_2 should not envy θ_1's allocation, so we should have

$$u(\theta_2) - C(e_2^*, \theta_2) \geq u(\theta_1) - C(0, \theta_2)$$

which implies that e_2^* should be smaller than some $\bar{e}$. Figure 4.1 shows one of the many wage functions that sustain such an equilibrium.[8]

4.2.2   Pooling Equilibria

In a pooling equilibrium, θ_1 and θ_2 choose the same diploma e^*; employers therefore have no reason to update their beliefs and offer a wage $\mu_0\theta_1 + (1 - \mu_0)\theta_2$. This configuration, however, is only possible when it gives the low-productivity agent as much as if he chose

---

8. Note that if e_2^* is high enough,

$$u(\theta_2) - C(e_2^*, \theta_2) < u(\mu_0\theta_1 + (1 - \mu_0)\theta_2) - C(0, \theta_2)$$

so the high-productivity agent will be better off if all schools close and there is no way to signal his productivity. Still, schools exist in this model and refusing to study will leave the high-productivity worker worse off.

not to study at all and to get wage θ_1. The diploma achieved in a pooling equilibrium therefore is bounded above by the $\bar{\bar{e}}$ such that

$$u(\mu_0\theta_1 + (1 - \mu_0)\theta_2) - C(\bar{\bar{e}}, \theta_1) = u(\theta_1) - C(0, \theta_1)$$

Note that in figure 4.2 when $e^* > 0$, all workers are better off if education is banned, since they then get the same wage $\mu_0\theta_1 + (1 - \mu_0)\theta_2$ and save the cost of going to school.

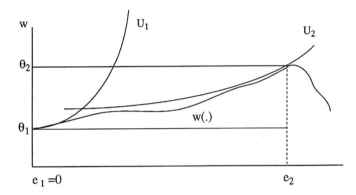

Figure 4.1
A separating equilibrium

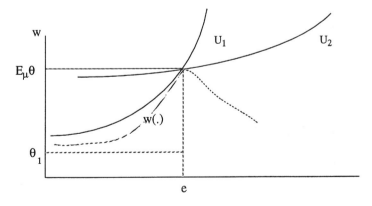

Figure 4.2
A pooling equilibrium

4.2.3   The Selection of an Equilibrium

There therefore exists a continuum of separating equilibria indexed by $e_2^* \in [\underline{e}, \bar{e}]$ and a continuum of pooling equilibria indexed by $e^* \in [0, \bar{e}]$. Employers make zero profits in all of these equilibria, since they compete à la Bertrand. On the other hand, the utility of employees decreases in e; the Pareto-optimum therefore is the pooling equilibrium where $e^* = 0$, and all other equilibria are Pareto-dominated by it.

This multiplicity of equilibria stems from the fact that out-of-equilibrium beliefs (i.e., the beliefs of employers on the productivity of an employee whose diploma is unusual) are not constrained by the definition of perfect Bayesian equilibria. The wage functions that employers offer therefore are only fixed for diplomas chosen in equilibrium; there are always out-of-equilibrium beliefs to sustain a given equilibrium, and this translates in the figures into the freedom we have to trace the graph of the function w^*. This type of equilibrium (where, we should note in passing, expectations are perfectly rational) gives rise to what are called *self-fulfilling prophecies*. It can moreover be shown that allowing education to affect productivity does not affect the multiplicity of equilibria.

There are two reasons why this multiplicity of equilibria is undesirable. The first one is that it severely limits the predictive power of the theory. The second one is that it makes comparative statics virtually impossible, since this favorite exercise of economists usually rests on the continuity of a locally unique equilibrium with respect to the primitives of the model.

The only way to reduce the number of equilibria and thus to obtain more precise predictions is to restrict the beliefs $\mu^*(e)$ (and therefore the wages $w^*(e)$) out of equilibrium. For instance, the wage functions I have drawn in figures 4.1 and 4.2 seem implausible, since they are lower for high diplomas. However, it would be easy to redraw the figures so that $w^*(e)$ increases in e at all ranges.

We need some stronger refinement if we are to select a unique equilibrium.

Happily, the "intuitive" criterion of Cho-Kreps (1987) allows us to eliminate all but one of these equilibria. First note that no pooling equilibrium satisfies the intuitive criterion. Let e^* be a pooling perfect Bayesian equilibrium, and let e be such that

$$u(\mu_0\theta_1 + (1 - \mu_0)\theta_2) - C(e^*, \theta_1) > u(\theta_2) - C(e, \theta_1)$$

Then deviating from e^* to e is a dominated strategy for θ_1: He can only obtain a low level of ability, even if all employers choose to believe that an agent who studies e years has high productivity and therefore should be offered wage θ_2. The intuitive criterion then says that we should have $\mu^*(e) = 0$ and $w^*(e) = \theta_2$ in such an e. But θ_2 then gains in forsaking e^* for the point designated by A on figure 4.3, and e^* cannot be an intuitive equilibrium. The same argument shows that the only separating equilibrium must leave θ_1 indifferent between $e = 0$ and $e = e_2^*$ (see figure 4.4).

Therefore the only intuitive equilibrium is the separating equilibrium that gives $e = 0$ and $w = \theta_1$ to the low-productivity agent and $e = \underline{e}$ and $w = \theta_2$ to the high-productivity agent, with

$$u(\theta_2) - C(\underline{e}, \theta_1) = u(\theta_1) - C(0, \theta_1)$$

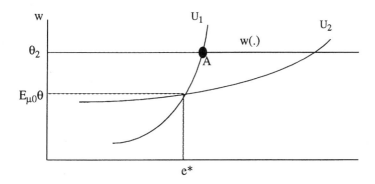

Figure 4.3
Pooling equilibria and the intuitive criterion

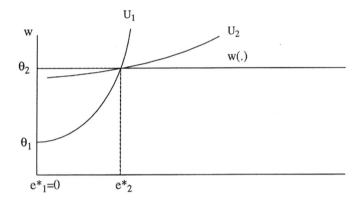

Figure 4.4
The intuitive equilibrium

  This equilibrium is called the *least-cost separating equilibrium,* since
the high-productivity agent chooses the minimum diploma that allows him to signal his type without attracting the low-productivity
agent. It is the most efficient separating perfect Bayesian equilibrium, in that it entails the least wasteful education. Moreover it does
not depend on the prior μ_0.
  This equilibrium is not unlike the optimum of adverse selection
models in some ways:[9]

• Only one of the two incentive constraints is active; it is the one that
prevents the low-productivity agent from posing as a high-productivity agent.

• Only one of the two types (the low-productivity agent) receives an
efficient allocation ($e = 0$).

Thus the results we get are in the end similar to those we obtained
for adverse selection models. However, we paid a price by using
refinements of perfect Bayesian equilibria that are still debated.

---

9. However, note that while adverse selection models typically lead to underproduction (of quality in the wine market example), Spence's model exhibits overpro-
duction (of education, which is a wasteful activity in this model).

4.3   Costless Signals

In Spence's model the fact that we can separate the agents (e.g., in the intuitive equilibrium) is due to the existence of a signal (education) whose cost varies with the type of the worker.

In fact Crawford-Sobel (1982) show that we can obtain semiseparating equilibria (and also nonseparating equilibria) even if the signal has no cost for the agent who sends it. Their model belongs to the cheap talk family: Since sending whatever signal is costless, it seems a priori that meaningful communication between the agents will be very difficult to achieve. The surprising result in this section is that while there always exists a *babbling* equilibrium in which signals convey no information whatsoever, there also exist equilibria that reveal some information.

I first present a simple example of how preplay communication can enhance the efficiency of an interaction. I then present the Crawford-Sobel model.

4.3.1   A Simple Example

Consider N villagers $i = 1, ..., N$, each of whom is privately informed of the cost he must incur if he goes hunting with the pack.[10] This cost, denoted c_i, is a priori uniformly distributed on $[0, 1 + \varepsilon]$, where ε is some positive number, and the c_i are independently distributed across villagers. If all agree to hunt together, they will catch a stag, which yields a value 1 to each of them. On the other hand, if only one villager decides to stay at home, the others will not be able to catch the stag.[11]

---

10. This cost may depend on his second-best options, such as growing food or caring for children.

11. This "stag hunt" story goes back to Jean-Jacques Rousseau, who used it in 1755 to illustrate the conflict between individualism and the need for cooperation in primitive societies.

Clearly the N villagers face a coordination problem: The risk for hunter i is that he goes hunting, incurs cost c_i and gets 0 value because one of his fellows has preferred to stay at home. In fact no one will hunt in the only Nash equilibrium of this game. To see this, let π be the equilibrium probability that any villager goes hunting. Then the expected value of going hunting to villager i is just the probability that all other villagers go hunting, which is π^{N-1}, and he will go hunting if and only if his private cost c_i is lower than π^{N-1}. This defines a *cutoff rule* according to which any villager decides to go hunting if and only if his private cost is lower than $c = \pi^{N-1}$. But in equilibrium it must be that π is just the probability that c_i is lower than c, which yields the equation

$$\pi = \frac{c}{1+\varepsilon} = \frac{\pi^{N-1}}{1+\varepsilon}$$

whose only solution clearly is $\pi = c = 0$. Thus no one will go hunting, which is very inefficient, since when ε is small, the probability that c_i is lower than 1 is close to 1.

Fortunately, a little preplay communication can improve things considerably. Let the game have two stages now:

· In the first stage each villager announces "yes" or "no" to all the others.

· Then each of them decides whether to go hunting.

I claim that this game has an equilibrium in which in the first stage, each villager announces "yes" if and only if his private cost c_i is lower than 1, and then

· if all villagers announced "yes," they all go hunting;
· if at least one of them announced "no," nobody goes hunting.

This is easily seen by reasoning backward. Moreover this equilibrium is almost efficient for ε small, since then all go hunting with probability close to 1. The trick here is that each villager knows after stage one whether any of his fellows will defect and stay at home, so there is no risk that he will incur his private cost c_i and not catch the stag. Also note that the labels "yes" or "no" are purely conventional; they could be replaced with "yellow" or "blue" or anything else.

Finally, note that there also exists a babbling equilibrium which conveys no information: for instance, all hunters could say "yes" whatever their c_i's, and play a Nash equilibrium in the second stage which would generate the former "no hunting" result.

4.3.2 The General Model

Crawford-Sobel's model is more abstract and more general than Spence's, but it has the same basic structure. It introduces two agents[12] whom we will call the sender and the receiver. The sender S observes the state of the world, which is a parameter $m \in [0, 1]$; the receiver R only observes a signal $n \in [0, 1]$ that is sent to him by S and that may help him to refine his prior μ, a cumulative distribution function on the state of the world m.

After he receives the signal n, the receiver forms a posterior given by a conditional cumulative distribution function $r(m \mid n)$ on the state of the world; he then takes a decision $y(n)$ that affects the utilities of both agents $U^S(y, m)$ and $U^R(y, m)$.

I will assume that

- U^S is concave in y and has a maximum in $y = y^S(m)$, and y^S is increasing
- U^R is concave in y and has a maximum in $y = y^R(m)$ which differs from $y^S(m)$ for all m.

As an example, we might have

$$\begin{cases} U^S(y, m) = -(y - m)^2 \\ U^R(y, m) = -(y - m - a)^2 \end{cases}$$

---

12. Exercise 4.4 shows how to build an N sender-one receiver model that nests the stag hunt story.

where a is a constant, so that $y^S(m) = m$ and $y^R(m) = m + a$. I will come back to this example later.

The difference $\|y^S - y^R\|$ measures the divergence between the objectives of both agents; it will limit the possibilities for communicating: S will only want to reveal information to R if the latter then takes a decision that suits S well enough.

The "contract" here is purely implicit: The sender anticipates that the receiver will react to the signal n by the decision $y(n)$ just because it is in the receiver's interest.

The perfect Bayesian equilibria of this game consist of a vector of strategies (y^*, q^*) and a system of beliefs r^* such that:

- S anticipates that if he sends the signal n, R will choose $y = y^*(n)$; he therefore sends $n = q^*(m) \in \arg\max_n U^S(y^*(n), m)$.

- When R observes a $n \in q^*([0, 1])$, first he forms a posterior $r^*(m \mid n)$, which he computes by restricting the prior μ to the set of states of the world that may have led S to send n, that is, $(q^*)^{-1}(n)$; then he chooses

$$y = y^*(n) \in \arg\max_y \int_0^1 U^R(y, m)\, dr^*(m \mid n)$$

or, equivalently,

$$y = y^*(n) \in \arg\max_y \int_{(q^*)^{-1}(n)} U^R(y, m)\, d\mu(m)$$

We will focus on "partition equilibria" in which the interval $[0, 1]$ is divided into p subintervals (which we denote $[m_{i-1}, m_i]$ for $i = 1, \ldots, p$, with $m_0 = 0$ and $m_p = 1$) and where the signal sent by the sender only depends on the subinterval the state of the world happens to be in:

$$\exists n_1 < \ldots < n_p, \quad \forall i = 1, \ldots, p, \quad q^*([m_{i-1}, m_i]) = \{n_i\}$$

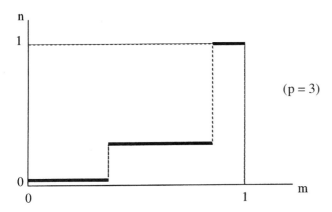

Figure 4.5
A partition equilibrium

It can be shown that all other perfect Bayesian equilibria can be turned into a partition equilibrium by a change of variables that does not change the economic interpretation of the results. More precisely, we can associate to each equilibrium a partition of $[0, 1]$ into $(A_1, \ldots, A_p)$ such that

$$\forall i = 1, \ldots, p, \quad q^*(A_i) = \{n_i\}$$

where the sequence $(n_1, \ldots, n_p)$ may not be increasing.

Crawford and Sobel show that there exists an integer N such that for all $p = 1, \ldots, N$, there is a partition equilibrium with p subintervals. Figure 4.5 shows such an equilibrium for the case where $p = 3$.

To see how these equilibria are determined, let us come back to the example given above in which utilities are quadratic and assume that the prior μ is the uniform distribution on $[0, 1]$. For a given sequence m_i, the receiver who gets the signal n_i maximizes over y,

$$\int_{m_{i-1}}^{m_i} -(y - m - a)^2 \, dm$$

which gives immediately

$$y_i = y^*(n_i) = \frac{m_{i-1} + m_i}{2} + a$$

Given the shape of the sender's utility function, the limit conditions

$$\forall i = 1, ..., p - 1, \quad U^S(y_{i+1}, m_i) = U^S(y_i, m_i)$$

will guarantee that he sends n_i if $m \in [m_{i-1}, m_i]$. But these conditions give

$$\left(\frac{m_{i-1} - m_i}{2} + a\right)^2 = \left(\frac{m_{i+1} - m_i}{2} + a\right)^2$$

whence

$$m_{i+1} = 2m_i - m_{i-1} - 4a$$

The solution to this difference equation must take the form $m_i = \lambda i^2 + \mu i + \nu$. The difference equation gives $\lambda = -2a$, and the initial and final conditions $m_0 = 0$ and $m_p = 1$ give $\nu = 0$ and $\mu = 1/p + 2ap$. We thus get the solution

$$m_i = \left(\frac{1}{p} + 2ap\right)i - 2ai^2$$

The sequence (m_i) must be increasing for this solution to be valid. Assume, for instance, that a is positive. Then we can rewrite the difference equation as

$$m_{i+1} - m_i = m_i - m_{i-1} - 4a$$

and therefore the sequence $(m_0, ..., m_p)$ is increasing if and only if

$$m_1 - m_0 - 4a(p - 1) > 0$$

or finally

$$\frac{1}{p} - 2ap + 2a > 0$$

As the left-hand side of this inequality decreases in p and goes to $-\infty$ in $+\infty$, it defines an integer N such that the sequence increases if and only if $p \leq N$.

This example exhibits all the properties of the Crawford-Sobel model. It shows that there always exists a noninformative equilibrium, which is again the babbling equilibrium: When $p = 1$, the sender sends a message that does not depend on the state of the world and the receiver does not change his prior.

The informativeness of the signal depends on the number p; in our example, this number can take all values from 1 to an integer N that increases when the absolute value of a decreases. There are therefore N more and more informative equilibria, up until the N-partition equilibria, which reveals the most information. It can be shown that this N-partition equilibrium Pareto-dominates all others, since it allows the players to coordinate on a more appropriate action. The closer the utilities (the smaller $|a|$), the higher is N: The informativeness of the equilibrium is only limited by the divergence of the players' objectives.

It bears emphasis that the signal is purely extrinsic here: It has no relationship with the primitives of the model. It is another case of what we call a cheap talk model. Instead of exchanging a signal in $[0, 1]$, the players could perfectly well communicate through an entirely different code. What matters is that the receiver can build up a scheme of interpretation in ways that reflect a preplay communication game. The minimum requirement for this is that the players have a common language that they use to agree on the description of the game.

4.4   Other Examples

It is usually difficult for the buyer of a good to form an opinion on its reliability, since that often only shows with experience. A seller who wants to draw the attention of the buyers to the reliability of his product can, however, announce that his product is covered by a warranty. This policy brings costs due to the maintenance and repair of the product, but these costs are low when the good indeed is reliable. The underlying model therefore is formally analogous to that of Spence;[13] thus offering warranties solves the Akerlof paradox studied at the beginning of this chapter. In the Cho-Kreps "intuitive" equilibrium, those sellers whose product is not reliable do not offer a warranty at all and those whose product is reliable offer the minimum warranty that allows them to separate from their competitors.

Leland-Pyle (1977) is another example of a signaling model à la Spence. They consider risk-averse entrepreneurs who want to finance risky projects. Each entrepreneur is privately informed of the expected return μ on his project. By retaining some equity in the project, an entrepreneur increases his exposure to risk but also his expected profits, and the latter effect is greater when μ is large. Thus entrepreneurs with higher-quality projects may signal their type by retaining a larger fraction of equity in their projects.

A journalist in the financial press who has had rosy inside information on the profits of a firm may be tempted to advise his readers to sell this firm's shares; if his readers follow his advice, the price of the shares will drop, and he will be able to buy cheap shares, to resell them after the high profits are announced, and thus to achieve some capital gain. This scenario can be reinterpreted inside the Crawford-Sobel model; the to-be-announced profits of the firm represent the state of the world m, the information published by the journalist (the sender) is the signal n, and the decision y taken by the readers (the collective receiver) is the number of shares they buy. If nothing limits the greed of the journalist, his objective is totally antagonistic to those of the readers, since their losses are his profits. Thus the only equilibrium of the game will be noninformative, with the readers

---

13. This similarity can be seen by replacing the type θ with the reliability of the product, the signal e with the characteristics of the warranty, and the wage w with the price of the good.

putting no trust at all in the journalist. The only way the journalist can use his privileged information is by sometimes telling the truth so that he can acquire a reputation for honesty. The conflict between the journalist's greed and his desire to be credible will determine how close his objectives and those of the readers become; this in turn will determine the maximum quantity of information that will be transmitted in equilibrium.[14]

4.5   The Informed Principal

To conclude this chapter, let us return to the informed Principal model. This clearly has close links with signaling models, since in both cases the party who moves first is informed. We studied in chapter 3 the case of private values; then the private characteristic of the Principal did not directly concern the Agent, and when the utilities were quasi-linear, the Principal therefore had nothing to gain by revealing his type. In Spence's model, for instance, the private characteristic of the worker is his productivity, and that influences the profits of the employer. Thus the analogous model is that of the informed Principal with common values. The worker then acts as the Principal and the employer as the Agent, and it clearly is important for the Principal that he can signal his type to the Agent. The game both parties play is, however, not quite the same as that we analyzed in this chapter, since the signal (education) is chosen before the wage contract is signed in Spence's model and after it is signed in the informed Principal model with common values. This explains why our results differ from those obtained by Maskin-Tirole (1992). Note, however, that the least-cost separating equilibrium plays an important role in both cases: In Spence's model, it is the only intuitive equilibrium; in Maskin-Tirole, it is the lower bound (for the Pareto criterion) of the set of equilibrium allocations.[15]

---

14. A variant of this model is studied in Benabou-Laroque (1992).
15. This set may reduce to a singleton if the prior probability of the low type is high enough.

Exercises

Exercise 4.1

Show, by using figures, that the Spence model has two types of semi-separating equilibria:

· Equilibria in which θ_1 chooses an education level e_1 and θ_2 randomizes between e_1 and a higher education level e_2.

· Equilibria in which θ_2 chooses an education level e_2 and θ_1 randomizes between e_2 and a lower education level e_1.

Exercise 4.2

In Spence's model, show that all perfect Bayesian equilibria are sequential (use the definition of sequential equilibria in the appendix to exhibit appropriate supporting beliefs).

Exercise 4.3

Show that the "intuitive" criterion eliminates all semiseparating equilibria in Spence's model.

Exercise 4.4

Consider a variant of the Crawford-Sobel model in which there are N senders $i = 1, \ldots, N$ and one receiver, with utility functions

$$U_i^S(y, m_i) = y(1 - m_i)$$

$$U^R(y, m_1, \ldots, m_N) = \sum_{i=1}^{N} U_i^S(y, m_i)$$

where y is a 0–1 variable. The prior on m_i is independently distributed as a uniform distribution on $[0, 1 + \varepsilon]$.

1. How does this fit the stag hunt story? (*Hint:* The receiver is the benevolent chief of the village, and $y = 1$ if and only if he has decided to send everybody hunting.)

2. Given what we saw in section 4.3.1, it seems reasonable to look for equilibria in which each sender i announces "yes" if and only if $m_i \leq m$ and "no" otherwise. Show that in any such equilibrium, there cannot be a switch from $y = 1$ to $y = 0$ if one villager changes his "no" to a "yes."

3. Show that m must be equal to 1.

4. (*Slightly more involved*) Compute the equilibrium probability that all go hunting and show that it converges to 1 as ε becomes arbitrarily small.

References

Akerlof, G. 1970. The market for lemons: Quality uncertainty and the market mechanism. *Quarterly Journal of Economics* 89:488–500.

Benabou, R., and G. Laroque. 1992. Using privileged information to manipulate markets: Insiders, gurus, and credibility. *Quarterly Journal of Economics* 107:921–58.

Cho, I.-K., and D. Kreps. 1987. Signaling games and stable equilibria. *Quarterly Journal of Economics* 102:179–221.

Crawford, V., and J. Sobel. 1982. Strategic information transmission. *Econometrica* 50:1431–51.

Leland, H., and D. Pyle. 1977. Asymmetries, financial structure, and financial intermediation. *Journal of Finance* 32:371–87.

Mas-Colell, A., M. Whinston, and J. Green. 1995. *Microeconomic Theory.* Oxford: Oxford University Press.

Maskin, E., and J. Tirole. 1992. The Principal-Agent relationship with an informed principal. II: Common values. *Econometrica* 60:1–42.

Spence, M. 1973. Job market signaling. *Quarterly Journal of Economics* 87:355–74.

5   Moral Hazard

Well, then, says I, what's the use you learning to do right when it's troublesome to do right and ain't no trouble to do wrong, and the wages is just the same? I was stuck. I couldn't answer that. So I reckoned I wouldn't bother no more about it, but afterwards always do whichever come handiest at the time.

Mark Twain, *Adventures of Huckleberry Finn.*[1]

We speak of *moral hazard* when

• the Agent takes a decision ("action") that affects his utility and that of the Principal;

• the Principal only observes the "outcome," an imperfect signal of the action taken;

• the action the Agent would choose spontaneously is not Pareto-optimal.

Since the action is unobservable, the Principal cannot force the Agent to choose an action that is Pareto-optimal. He can only influence the choice of an action by the Agent by conditioning the Agent's utility to the only variable that is observable: the outcome. This in turn can only be done by giving the Agent a transfer that depends on the outcome.

Examples of moral hazard abound; in fact it is somewhat difficult to imagine an economic relationship that is not contaminated by this

---

1. Quoted by Holmstrom-Milgrom (1987).

problem.[2] If such a relationship existed, then the Principal would be able to observe perfectly all the decision variables of the Agent that affect his utility; this would require extremely costly supervision efforts.

Moral hazard appears everywhere inside firms, given that employers rarely can control all decisions of their employees. The term *effort* is often used to designate all employee inputs that are not directly observable; the employer can only condition wages on production or on other observable variables to induce employees to put in effort. This term is confusing in that it seems to suggest that the only moral hazard problem in firms consists in getting employees to work; in fact there will be moral hazard as soon as the objectives of the parties differ. A good example is that of relationships between shareholders and managers; the latter, being autonomous agents, will have their own objectives which may not identify with those of the shareholders (who above all want the firm's value to be maximized).

In the case of property insurance, the moral hazard aspect stems from the fact that the insurer cannot observe the self-protection efforts (precautions against theft, fire, etc.) of the insured, even though these positively affect his profits.

There is also moral hazard in all service activities, where the effort of the service provider affects the outcome of his task. Simple examples include the relationship between a car-owner and his mechanic, or between a patient and his doctor.

Finally, moral hazard is often studied in the economics of development to describe the relationships between landowners and their farmers: sharecropping agreements indeed stipulate that the harvest will be shared between both parties, thus making it important for the landlord to get the farmer to put in effort.

The first-best situation is defined by the assumption that the Principal can observe the Agent's action. In that case he can order the

---

2. The moral hazard model actually is often called the "agency problem" and then identified with the Principal-Agent model.

Agent to choose the efficient action,[3] and then choose the wages that achieve the optimal risk sharing.

In particular, it is often assumed in these models that the Principal is risk-neutral; this is justified in the usual way by assuming that the Principal faces many independent risks and thus can diversify the risks associated to his relationship with the Agent.[4] On the other hand, the Agent normally exhibits risk-aversion (being "small," it is more difficult for him to diversify his risks). Optimal risk sharing then implies that the Principal perfectly insures the Agent by giving him a constant wage and by bearing all risks involved in their common activity.

In the second-best situation we are concerned with, the Principal can only observe a variable correlated with the Agent's action: the outcome. We just saw that if the Principal is risk-neutral, the first-best optimum consists in giving the Agent a constant wage; but in second-best circumstances, this induces the Agent to choose selfishly the action that is the least costly for him, and this in general is not optimal.[5] Solving the moral hazard problem thus implies that the Principal offers the Agent a contract that trades off

• risk sharing, which suggests that the Agent's wage should not depend too strongly on the outcome;

• incentives, which induce the Principal to condition the Agent's wage on the outcome.

Thus we find here the same sort of trade-off as in adverse selection models, where the problem was to give the Agent enough incentives without increasing his rent too much.

Note that when the Agent is risk-neutral, the trade-off disappears: He can bear all the risks, and the second-best coincides with the

---

3. Or, equivalently, the Principal can fine the Agent if he does not choose the efficient action.
4. This is by no means always the most natural assumption, as the patient-doctor relationship shows. However, it is not crucial to the analysis.
5. This is the meaning of the *Huckleberry Finn* quotation that opens this chapter.

first-best, in which risk-sharing is irrelevant. We sometimes say in that case that the moral hazard problem is solved by "selling the firm to the Agent." However, this case has little practical interest.

5.1   A Simple Example

Let us start with the simplest framework: a two action, two outcome model. The Agent can choose between working ($a = 1$) and not working ($a = 0$). The cost of action a is normalized to a so that the Agent's utility if he gets wage w and chooses action a is ($u(w) - a$), where u is strictly concave. The only thing the Principal can observe is whether the Agent succeeds or fails at his task. If the Agent works, his probability of succeeding is P and the Principal then gets a payoff x_S. If he does not work, the probability of success falls to $p < P$. The Principal's payoff in case of failure is $x_F < x_S$.

The interesting case is where the Principal wants the Agent to work. Then he must give the Agent wages w_S (in case of success) and w_F (in case of failure) such that it pays the Agent to work:

$$Pu(w_S) + (1 - P)u(w_F) - 1 \geq pu(w_S) + (1 - p)u(w_F)$$

which yields the incentive constraint

$$(P - p)(u(w_S) - u(w_F)) \geq 1$$

Thus the Principal must (obviously) give the Agent a higher wage when he works, and the difference ($w_S - w_F$) increases when P gets closer to p so that it becomes more difficult to distinguish a worker from a nonworker: We then say that the incentives become more *high powered*.

We must also take into account an individual rationality constraint that states that the Agent finds it more worthwhile to work than to quit and get his outside option $\underline{U}$. This gives

$$Pu(w_S) + (1 - P)u(w_F) - 1 \geq \underline{U}$$

Clearly this last inequality must be an equality; otherwise the Principal could decrease both w_S and w_F by the same small transfer ε, which would not affect the incentive constraint and would increase his own utility, since (assuming he is risk-neutral) this is

$$P(x_S - w_S) + (1 - P)(x_F - w_F)$$

Proving that the incentive constraint is an equality is slightly more involved. If it were a strict inequality, then we could subtract $(1 - P)\varepsilon/u'(w_S)$ from w_S and add $P\varepsilon/u'(w_F)$ to w_F. The incentive constraint would still hold for ε small, and by construction, $u(w_S)$ would decrease by $(1 - P)\varepsilon$ and $u(w_F)$ would increase by $P\varepsilon$ so that the individual rationality constraint would still be satisfied. Moreover the wage bill $(Pw_S + (1 - P)w_F)$ of the Principal would decrease by $P(1 - P)\varepsilon(1/u'(w_S) - 1/u'(w_F))$, which is positive, since $w_F < w_S$ and u is strictly concave.[6]

Since both inequalities are in fact linear equalities in $(u(w_F), u(w_S))$ and we have just two unknowns, it is easy to solve for $u(w_S)$ and $u(w_F)$. This gives

$$\begin{cases} u(w_F) = \underline{U} - \dfrac{p}{P - p} \\ u(w_S) = \underline{U} + \dfrac{1 - p}{P - p} \end{cases}$$

from which we could easily compute the Principal's expected utility

$$W_1 = P(x_S - w_S) + (1 - P)(x_F - w_F)$$

Note that in this very special case, we only relied on the maximization of W_1 to prove that both constraints should be binding at the optimum.

Of course it might be that the Principal finds it too costly to get the Agent to work and decides to let him shirk instead. In that case he

---

6. More diagram-oriented readers can also easily see this by drawing a curve in the $(u(w_F), u(w_S))$ plane.

will give the Agent a constant wage $w_S = w_F = w$ such that $u(w)$ = $\underline{U}$, and he will get an expected utility

$$W_0 = px_S + (1 - p)x_F - w$$

Now the difference between W_0 and W_1 can be rewritten as

$$W_1 - W_0 = (P - p)(x_S - x_F) + w - Pw_S - (1 - P)w_F$$

and since the wages do not depend on x_S and x_F, it appears that if success is much more attractive than failure for the Principal ($x_S - x_F$ is high), then he will choose to get the Agent to work. The reader is asked in exercise 5.1 to prove that if this is the case, then $x_S - w_S > x_F - w_F$ at the optimum, with the surplus from success shared between the Agent and the Principal.

5.2   The Standard Model

Let us also consider the standard model in a discrete version. The Agent must choose between n possible actions: $a_1, \ldots, a_n$. These actions produce one among m outcomes, which we may denote $x_1, \ldots, x_m$.

The outcome a priori is only a signal that brings information on the action the Agent chooses. To simplify matters, let us identify it here with the surplus from the relationship.[7] We will return to this assumption in section 5.3.4.

The stochastic relationship between actions and outcomes is often called a "technology." Let us assume that when the Agent chooses the action a_i, the Principal observes the outcome x_j with a probability p_{ij} that is positive.[8]

---

7. For instance, in an employer-employee relationship, a will be the effort and x the resulting production or profit.

8. If some of the probabilities p_{ij} were zero, the Principal could use this information to exclude some actions. Assume, for instance, that action a_i is the first-best optimal action and that $p_{ij} = 0$ for some j. The Principal then could fine the Agent heavily when the outcome is x_j, since the fact that he observes x_j signals that the Agent did not choose the optimum action a_i. This type of strategy may even allow the Principal

The only variable that is publicly observed is the outcome; thus contracts must take the form of a wage that only depends on the outcome. If the Principal observes the outcome x_j, he will pay the Agent a wage w_j and keep $(x_j - w_j)$ for himself.

A general specification for the Agent's von Neumann–Morgenstern utility function would be $u(w, a)$. However, the choice of action would then affect the agent's preferences toward risk, which would needlessly complicate the analysis. Therefore we will assume that the Agent's utility is separable in income and action. Moreover it is always possible to renormalize the actions so that their marginal cost is constant. Thus I will take the Agent's utility function to be

$$u(w) - a$$

where u is increasing and concave.

As in most of the literature, we will assume that the Principal is risk-neutral. His von Neumann–Morgenstern utility function then is

$$x - w$$

5.2.1   The Agent's Program

When the Principal offers him a contract (w_j), the Agent chooses his action by solving the following program:

$$\max_{i=1,\ldots,n} \left(\sum_{j=1}^{m} p_{ij} u(w_j) - a_i \right)$$

If the Agent chooses a_i, then the $(n - 1)$ incentive constraints

$$\sum_{j=1}^{m} p_{ij} u(w_j) - a_i \geq \sum_{j=1}^{m} p_{kj} u(w_j) - a_k \quad (IC_k)$$

must hold for $k = 1, \ldots, n$ and $k \neq i$.

---

to implement the first-best: if moreover $p_{kj} > 0$ for all $k \neq i$, then the choice of any a_k other than a_i would expose the Agent to a large fine, thus effectively deterring him from deviating. For this reason, I exclude this case.

However, the Agent will accept the contract only if it gives him a utility no smaller than some $\underline{U}$ that represents the utility the Agent can obtain by breaking his relationship with the Principal (his next-best opportunity). The participation constraint (the individual rationality constraint) thus can be written

$$\sum_{j=1}^{m} p_{ij}u(w_j) - a_i \geq \underline{U} \quad (IR)$$

if the Agent's preferred action is a_i.

5.2.2   The Principal's Program

The Principal should choose the contract $(w_1, \ldots, w_m)$ that maximizes his expected utility, while taking into account the consequences of this contract on the Agent's decisions:

$$\max_{(w_1, \ldots, w_m), i} \sum_{j=1}^{m} p_{ij}(x_j - w_j)$$

under

$$\begin{cases} (IC_k) & k = 1, \ldots, n \text{ and } k \neq i \quad (\lambda_k) \\ (IR) & (\mu) \end{cases}$$

where a_i is the action chosen at the optimum and the numbers in parentheses represent the (nonnegative) multipliers associated with the constraints. Note that the maximization is with respect to the wages (w_j) but also to the action a_i, whose choice the Principal indirectly controls.

Let us fix a_i; the Lagrangian of the maximization problem is

$$\mathcal{L}(w, \lambda, \mu) = \sum_{j=1}^{m} p_{ij}(x_j - w_j) + \sum_{k=1; k \neq i}^{n} \lambda_k \left(\sum_{j=1}^{m} p_{ij}u(w_j) - a_i \right.$$
$$\left. - \sum_{j=1}^{m} p_{kj}u(w_j) + a_k \right) + \mu \left(\sum_{j=1}^{m} p_{ij}u(w_j) - a_i - \underline{U} \right)$$

Differentiating it with respect to w_j and regrouping terms yields

$$\frac{1}{u'(w_j)} = \mu + \sum_{k=1,k\neq i}^{n} \lambda_k \left(1 - \frac{p_{kj}}{p_{ij}}\right) \qquad (E)$$

At the first-best, we would get the efficient risk-sharing; the ratio of marginal utilities of the Principal and the Agent would be constant, which implies that the wage itself is constant:

$$\frac{1}{u'(w_j)} = \mu_0$$

where μ_0 is chosen so that the constraint (IR) is an equality.

The difference between these two equations comes from the fact that some multipliers λ_k may be positive. That is, some incentive constraints may be active, so some actions a_k give the Agent the same expected utility as a_i. In equilibrium at least one of the λ_k must be positive (otherwise, we could neglect the incentive constraints, and the moral hazard problem would vanish); w_j then depends on j through the terms p_{kj}/p_{ij}.

The p_{kj}/p_{ij} terms play a fundamental role in the analysis of the moral hazard problem. They can be interpreted through an analogy with mathematical statistics. The Principal's problem indeed consists in part in trying to infer the action the Agent chose from the observation of the outcome. In statistical terms the Principal wants to estimate the "parameter" a from the observation of the "sample" x. This can be solved by computing the maximum likelihood estimator, which is the a_k such that k maximizes the probability p_{kj}. The following two statements are therefore equivalent:

a_i is the maximum likelihood estimator of a given x_j

and

$$\forall k, \quad \frac{p_{kj}}{p_{ij}} \leq 1$$

For this reason the p_{kj}/p_{ij} quantities are called "likelihood ratios." This analogy allows us to interpret equation (E). Again, fix the optimal action a_i; since all multipliers λ_k are nonnegative and the function $1/u'$ is increasing, the wage w_j associated with outcome j will tend to be higher when a greater number of likelihood ratios p_{kj}/p_{ij} are smaller than 1. This wage will therefore tend to be higher when a_i is the maximum likelihood estimator of a given x_j. Of course this argument is not airtight, since the wage w_j depends on a *weighted* sum of the likelihood ratios.[9] Still, the intuition is important and basically right: The Principal will give the Agent a high wage when he observes an outcome that leads him to infer that the action taken was the optimal one; on the other hand, he will give the Agent a low wage if the outcome makes it very unlikely that the Agent chose the optimal action.

Before we study the properties of the optimal contract, let us consider briefly an alternative approach popularized by Grossman-Hart (1983). They solve the Principal's maximization program in two stages:

• For any action a_i, they minimize the cost to implement it for the Principal. This amounts to minimizing the wage bill

$$\sum_{j=1}^{m} p_{ij} w_j$$

under the incentive constraints and the participation constraint.

• They then choose the action that maximizes the difference between the expected benefit from action a_i, or

$$\sum_{j=1}^{m} p_{ij} x_j$$

and the cost-minimizing wage bill.

---

9. The reader should check that with only two actions ($n = 2$), the argument holds as given in the text.

This is clearly equivalent to the approach used above. However, the Grossman-Hart approach may be more enlightening in some cases.

5.2.3   Properties of the Optimal Contract

Assume that $x_1 < \ldots < x_m$ and $a_1 < \ldots < a_n$; we will study here how the wage w_j depends on the outcome j. When the action is observable and the Principal is risk-neutral, w_j is constant; if, more generally, the Principal is risk-averse with a concave von Neumann-Morgenstern utility function v, then the ratios of marginal utilities

$$\frac{v'(x_j - w_j)}{u'(w_j)}$$

are independent of j at the first-best.[10] This clearly implies that the first-best wage w_j is an increasing function of j. This property seems to be desirable for the second-best wage schedule: It seems natural that the wage should be higher when the surplus to be shared is higher, and we did obtain such a result for the two action, two outcome example in section 5.1. Can we get such a conclusion here?

It turns out that the answer is quite disappointing. In the general case, it is only possible to show that (see Grossman-Hart 1983)

1. w_j cannot be uniformly decreasing in j,

2. neither can $(x_j - w_j)$,

3. $\exists (j, l), w_j > w_l$ and $x_j - w_j \geq x_l - w_l$.

These results, whose proof is fairly complex and will be omitted here, are obviously very weak and very remote from what our still untrained intuition suggests. We cannot exclude, for instance, an optimal wage schedule that would actually decrease on part of the range. The only case in which these three results provide a positive answer is that when there are only two possible outcomes (e.g., success or failure). The optimal wage schedule can then be written

---

10. This is known in the literature as Borch's rule.

$$\begin{cases} w_1 = w \\ w_2 = w + s(x_2 - x_1) \end{cases}$$

so that the Agent receives a basis wage w and a bonus proportional to the increase in the surplus when he succeeded. Part 3 of the result given above shows that the bonus rate s must satisfy $0 < s \le 1$: Wages increase with the outcome, but not so fast that they exhaust the whole increase in the surplus.

When there are more than two outcomes, we cannot obtain more positive results without putting more structure on the technology that produces the outcome (the probabilities p_{ij}). The outcome indeed plays a dual role in this model: It represents the global surplus to be shared, but it is also a signal that informs the Principal on the action chosen by the Agent. The informative properties of this signal determine the shape of the solution, such as was already apparent in our discussion of the likelihood ratios.

Let us come back to (E), the equation that defines the optimal contract:

$$\frac{1}{u'(w_j)} = \mu + \sum_{k=1, k \ne i}^{n} \lambda_k \left(1 - \frac{p_{kj}}{p_{ij}} \right)$$

As the left-hand side of (E) increases in w_j, w_j will increase in j if and only if the right-hand side of (E) itself increases in j. We just have to find conditions that ensure that such is the case. To do this, first assume that a high action increases the probability of getting a high outcome at least as much as it increases the probability of getting a low outcome:

$$\forall k < i, \forall l < j, \quad \frac{p_{ij}}{p_{il}} \ge \frac{p_{kj}}{p_{kl}}$$

This condition amounts to assuming that for all $k < i$, the likelihood ratio p_{ij}/p_{kj} increases with the outcome j; it is called the *monotone likelihood ratio condition* (MLRC).

Let us compare the MLRC to another commonly used way of comparing probability distributions, first-order stochastic dominance. Denote $P_{ij} = \sum_{l=1}^{j} p_{il}$ the cumulative distribution function of the outcome conditionally on the action a. First-order stochastic dominance states that this cumulative distribution function moves to the right as a increases, which means that P_{ij} decreases in i for all j. In other words, however one defines a good outcome, the probability of a good outcome increases in a. This implies, inter alia, that the expected outcome $\sum_{j=1}^{m} p_{ij} x_j$ increases with the action a_i. To see this, just note that

$$\sum_{j=1}^{m} p_{ij} x_j = P_{i1} x_1 + \sum_{j=2}^{m} (P_{ij} - P_{i,j-1}) x_j$$

$$= \sum_{j=1}^{m-1} P_{ij}(x_j - x_{j+1}) + x_m$$

Now, since $x_j < x_{j+1}$ and P_{ij} decreases in i, then the expected outcome increases in i.

It can easily be shown that MLRC and first-order stochastic dominance are equivalent if there are only two possible outcomes. In the general case, MLRC still implies first-order stochastic dominance. Take indeed $k < i$. By MLRC, the likelihood ratio p_{kj}/p_{ij} is an increasing function of j. Moreover this ratio cannot be always greater than 1, or we would have

$$1 = \sum_{j=1}^{m} p_{ij} = \sum_{j=1}^{m} p_{kj} \frac{p_{ij}}{p_{kj}} > \sum_{j=1}^{m} p_{kj} = 1$$

which is absurd. There must therefore exist an index q such that

$$q = \max \left\{ j = 1, ..., m \mid \frac{p_{ij}}{p_{kj}} \leq 1 \right\}$$

Now consider the function defined by $F_0 = 0$ and

$\forall j = 1, \ldots, m, \quad F_j = P_{kj} - P_{ij}$

Note that $F_m = 0$. We have

$$\forall j = 1, \ldots, m, \quad F_j - F_{j-1} = p_{kj} - p_{ij} = p_{kj}\left(1 - \frac{p_{ij}}{p_{kj}}\right)$$

so F_j increases in j for $j \le q$ and decreases in j for $q < j \le m$. But since $F_0 = F_m = 0$, we must have $F_j \ge 0$ for all j, which proves first-order stochastic dominance.

Since the multipliers λ_k are nonnegative, MLRC allows us to state that the $\lambda_k(1 - p_{kj}/p_{ij})$ terms in (E) are increasing in j if $k < i$, and decreasing otherwise. We will therefore be done if we can find a condition that implies that the multipliers λ_k are all zero when k is greater than i, that is, that the only active incentive constraints are those that prevent the Agent from choosing actions less costly than the optimal action.

Note that if $i = n$, in which case the Principal wants to implement the most costly action, then we are done. Thus when there are only two possible actions (as when the choice is work–do not work) and the Principal wants the Agent to work, the MLRC is enough to ensure that the wage increases in the outcome. In the general case Grossman and Hart proposed[11] the *convexity of the distribution function condition* (CDFC).[12] This new condition states that the cumulative distribution function of the outcome is convex in a on $\{a_1, \ldots, a_n\}$. More precisely, for $i < j < k$ and $\lambda \in [0, 1]$ such that

$a_j = \lambda a_i + (1 - \lambda)a_k$

CDFC says that

$\forall l = 1, \ldots, m, \quad P_{jl} \le \lambda P_{il} + (1 - \lambda)P_{kl}$

---

11. Both (MLRC) and (CDFC) in fact appear in earlier work by Mirrlees.
12. Confusingly, some authors call it the *concavity of the distribution function condition,* meaning that the *decumulated* distribution function (one minus the cumulative distribution function) is concave.

One rough interpretation of the CDFC condition is that returns to the action are stochastically decreasing; however, this should be taken with a bit of skepticism. CDFC really has no clear economic interpretation, and its validity is much more doubtful than that of MLRC.[13] The main appeal of this condition is that it will allow us to obtain the result we seek, as we will now show.

Let a_i be the optimal action. It is easy to see that there must exist a $l < i$ such that the multiplier λ_l is positive. If all λ_k were zero for $k < i$, then the optimal wage would be the same if the choice of possible actions were restricted to $A = \{a_i, ..., a_n\}$. But the optimal wage would then be constant, since a_i is the least costly action in A. Now, a constant wage can only implement action a_1 and not a_i in the global problem, so this conclusion is absurd.

Consider the problem in which the Agent is restricted to choosing an action in $\{a_1, ..., a_i\}$, and let w be the optimal wage. In this problem a_i is the costliest action and MLRC therefore implies that w_j increases in j. We will show that w stays optimal if we allow the Agent to choose from the unrestricted set of actions $\{a_1, ..., a_n\}$. Assume, to the contrary, that there exists a $k > i$ such that the Agent prefers to choose a_k:

$$\sum_{j=1}^{m} p_{kj} u(w_j) - a_k > \sum_{j=1}^{m} p_{ij} u(w_j) - a_i$$

and let l be the index of an action less costly than a_i and whose associated multiplier λ_k is nonzero so that

$$\sum_{j=1}^{m} p_{lj} u(w_j) - a_l = \sum_{j=1}^{m} p_{ij} u(w_j) - a_i$$

There exists a $\lambda \in [0,1]$ such that

---

13. Take, for instance, a slightly different model in which there is a continuous set of outcomes given by $x = a + \varepsilon$, where ε is some random noise with probability distribution function f. Then returns to the action are clearly constant; however, CDFC is equivalent here to f being nondecreasing, not a very appealing property.

$a_i = \lambda a_k + (1 - \lambda)a_l$

and we can therefore apply CDFC:

$\forall j = 1, \ldots, m, \quad P_{ij} \leq \lambda P_{kj} + (1 - \lambda)P_{lj}$

We deduce from this

$$\sum_{j=1}^{m} p_{ij} u(w_j) - a_i = \sum_{j=1}^{m-1} P_{ij}(u(w_j) - u(w_{j+1})) + u(w_m) - a_i$$

$$\geq \lambda \left(\sum_{j=1}^{m-1} P_{kj}(u(w_j) - u(w_{j+1})) + u(w_m) - a_k \right)$$

$$+ (1 - \lambda) \left(\sum_{j=1}^{m-1} P_{lj}(u(w_j) - u(w_{j+1})) + u(w_m) - a_l \right)$$

$$= \lambda \left(\sum_{j=1}^{m} p_{kj} u(w_j) - a_k \right)$$

$$+ (1 - \lambda) \left(\sum_{j=1}^{m} p_{lj} u(w_j) - a_l \right)$$

which is absurd by the definition of a_k and a_l. The wage schedule w therefore is the optimal solution in the global problem, and this concludes our proof because w is increasing.

The general conclusion that should be drawn from this analysis is that the structure of the simplest moral hazard problem is already very rich and that it is therefore dangerous to trust one's intuition too much. It is not necessarily true, for instance, that the second-best optimal action is less costly for the Agent than the first-best optimal action. It may not be true either that the expected profit of the Principal increases when the Agent becomes more "productive" (in the sense of first-order stochastic dominance) whatever action he chooses.[14] The literature contains many negative results of this sort.

---

14. Exercise 5.3 provides a counterexample.

5.3 Extensions

5.3.1 Informativeness and Second-Best Loss

Since the Principal must provide incentives to the Agent, his expected profit is lower in the second-best than it is in the first-best. We will show here that this loss in utility is greater when the technology is less informative.

Consider an (m, m) stochastic matrix[15] R, and assume that the probabilities p transform into numbers p' such that

$$\forall i, j, \quad p'_{ij} = \sum_{k=1}^{m} R_{jk} p_{ik}$$

Clearly the p' also are probabilities, since each column of R sums to one. Let also the outcomes x transform into x' so that the expected surplus stays constant for each action:[16]

$$\forall i, \quad \sum_{j=1}^{m} p'_{ij} x'_j = \sum_{j=1}^{m} p_{ij} x_j$$

We can interpret this transformation by imagining the following two-step experiment: The Principal does not observe the outcome x_k obtained according to the distribution p_{ij} given the choice of an action a_i, but only an outcome x'_j that is obtained by drawing from the outcomes x' with the probability distribution associated with the kth column of R. This transformation of the probabilities thus corresponds to a lesser informativeness (a *coarsening*) in the sense of Blackwell: In statistical terms, inferences drawn on a after observing x' with probabilities p' will be less precise than those drawn from observing x when the probabilities are p.

---

15. A stochastic matrix is a square matrix such that all of its elements are nonnegative and the elements in each column sum to 1.
16. This can be achieved by letting $x' = Sx$, where S is the inverse of the transpose of R.

Let a_i be an action and w' a wage schedule that implements it in the (p', x') model. Now recall the (p, x) model, and consider the wage schedule w given by

$$u(w_j) = \sum_{k=1}^{m} R_{kj} u(w'_k)$$

Going back to the two-step experiment invoked above, it is easy to see that this wage schedule implements a_i in the (p, x) model. We have indeed

$$\sum_{j=1}^{m} p_{ij} u(w_j) = \sum_{j=1}^{m} \sum_{k=1}^{m} p_{ij} R_{kj} u(w'_k)$$

$$= \sum_{k=1}^{m} p'_{ik} u(w'_k)$$

Moreover this implementation is less costly for the Principal than that by w' in the (p', x') model, since it imposes less risk to the (risk-averse) Agent.

This result, which appears in both Gjesdal (1982) and Grossman-Hart (1983), shows that the optimal action can be implemented at less cost in the more informative model. Of course the relation "being more informative than" is only a very partial order in the set of possible technologies, and thus this result has little practical interest. However, it allows us to exhibit another of the many links between the moral hazard problem and the principles of statistical inference.

5.3.2 A Continuum of Actions

When a takes its values in a continuous interval $[\underline{a}, \bar{a}]$, the incentive constraints become too numerous to be really tractable. One must then use the "first-order approach," which consists in neglecting all nonlocal incentive constraints.

Let $p_j(a)$ be the probability of x_j given a; the Agent maximizes

$$\sum_{j=1}^{m} p_j(a)u(w_j) - a$$

in a so that at the first-order

$$\sum_{j=1}^{m} p_j'(a)u(w_j) = 1$$

The first-order approach consists in neglecting all other conditions: the local second-order condition

$$\sum_{j=1}^{m} p_j''(a)u(w_j) \leq 0$$

and the global conditions.

Models with a continuous set of actions were among the first considered in the literature. The question of the validity of the first-order approach thus featured prominently, even though it is after all only a technical point. Rogerson (1985) showed that this approach is valid under CDFC and MLRC, and that the wage then automatically increases with the outcome. Recall, however, that CDFC is not a particularly appealing condition; Jewitt (1988) proposed weaker conditions on technology at the cost of requiring new conditions on the Agent's utility function.

*5.3.3   An Infinity of Outcomes

Several papers have used an infinite (usually continuous) set of outcomes. Most of them did not prove the existence of an optimum, which is a tricky problem in that case: The contract w indeed becomes a function. Since the Principal maximizes with respect to w, he must therefore choose a function in a functional space. This problem belongs to functional analysis; it only has a solution (in general) if the objective is continuous in w (which raises no particular problem) and if the space in which the function w is chosen is compact. Unfortunately, most natural function spaces are not compact; one must impose restrictions on the shape of the contracts to keep a compact functional space (Page 1987). These restrictions (e.g., the equicontinuity of admissible w functions) unfortunately are not especially intuitive.

5.3.4 The Multisignal Case

The Principal may not only observe the outcome x that identifies to the global surplus but also a signal y that has no intrinsic economic value though it brings information on a. Thus an employer may observe the production of his employees but also get reports from middle management. How should the employer use this information?

Simple calculations show that (E) transforms into

$$\forall (j, y), \quad \frac{1}{u'(w_j^y)} = \mu + \sum_{k=1, k \neq i}^{n} \lambda_k \left(1 - \frac{p_{kj}^y}{p_{ij}^y} \right)$$

which characterizes the way the wage w depends on j and y (here p_{ij}^y denotes the probability of the pair (x_j, y) given a_i). The Principal will therefore condition the wage on y if and only if p_{kj}^y / p_{ij}^y depends on y; but that, in statistical terms, is exactly the definition for x not being a sufficient statistic of (x, y) for a.[17]

This property underlies the *sufficient statistic theorem* (see Holmstrom 1979): The Principal conditions the wage on a sufficient statistic for all the signals he receives, whether extrinsic or intrinsic. Thus the employer should condition wages on middle management reports as well as production if the reports convey information on the Agent's action that is not already contained in production.

---

17. Intuitively this just means that the pair (x, y) contains more information on a than x alone.

A recent paper by Kim (1995) generalizes both this result and the informativeness result of section 5.3.1 in the context of noninclusive information systems.

5.3.5   Models with Several Agents

In practice, it may difficult to isolate the interaction between the Principal and the Agent. If, for instance, the Principal is an employer and the Agent is his employee, the Principal will usually have similar relationships with other employees.

Such will be the case for teamwork. If the Agent works in a team and only the team's global production can be measured, then the Agent's wage can only depend on global production unless the Principal gets reports on each team member's effort. This clearly may induce Agents to free-ride on the effort of others, as proved by Holmstrom (1982). More generally, if a worker's effort additionally influences the production of some of his colleagues, then his wage should depend on their production as well as his own if individual production can be observed (Mookherjee 1984): This is a simple consequence of the sufficient statistic theorem.

Now consider a group of employees who accomplish similar tasks such that the production of each Agent depends on his effort, a noise that is common to all employees, and an idiosyncratic noise. Imagine, for instance, a group of workers who work in the same shop on partly independent tasks and who use the same machine tools; sellers of the same product to different clients also fit the picture. The sufficient statistic theorem then shows that the wage of each employee should depend on the productions of all, since observing all productions allows the employer to reduce uncertainty as to the common noise. As emphasized by Holmstrom (1982), competition among Agents here only has value insofar as it allows a better extraction of information by the Principal: If there were no common noise, then competition would be useless.

One frequently observes (especially in firms that rely on internal promotion) various practices of relative evaluation of employees that condition their utility on the way they are ranked by their superiors. This may be the only solution for the Principal if more specific measures of output are unverifiable. Green-Stokey (1983) have shown that in the model of the previous paragraph, these "tournaments" are almost optimal when there are many employees doing the same task; then the ranks of employees effectively become an almost sufficient statistic of their productions when employees are very numerous.

Finally, take different Agents whose tasks are affected by independent observational noises, but such that each Agent may spend some of his time helping his colleagues accomplish their tasks. If the wage given to Agent i only depends on how he accomplishes his own task, then he will not be induced to help his colleagues. However, it may be that the optimal contract consists in getting Agents to help each other. Itoh (1991) studies how the Principal can create the conditions for teamwork in such a model.

All these results assume that Agents adopt strategies that form a Nash equilibrium: Our conclusions might change drastically if the Agents were to coordinate their actions, by adopting collusive strategies for instance.

*5.3.6   The Robustness of Contracts

We have seen that the optimal wage schedule depends on the likelihood ratios, which are relatively fine characteristics of the technology. Moreover the sufficient statistic theorem indicates that the optimal wage should depend on all signals that may bring information on the action chosen by the Agent. Theory therefore suggests that the optimal incentive contract in moral hazard problems should be a complex nonlinear function of an a priori fairly large number of variables. This prediction does not accord well with experience;

real-life contracts appear to have a rather simple shape (they are often linear) and to depend on a small number of variables only.

Holmstrom-Milgrom (1987) have tried to break from this dead-lock by suggesting that simple (linear) contracts may be more robust than more complex contracts.[18] Their idea is that the complexity of the optimal contract in our models is due to the fact that the tech-nology the Agent owns is highly restricted. If the Agent is left much more freedom, then the shape of the optimal contract will be sim-pler. This is the essence of the argument; the rest of this section is mathematically involved and can be skipped.

To illustrate their argument, Holmstrom-Milgrom consider a con-tinuous-time model in which the outcome is produced by a diffu-sion process whose trend the Agent can control:

$$dx_t = a_t \, dt + \sigma \, dW_t$$

where W is a Brownian motion[19] and $t \in [0, 1]$. The choice space of the Agent is therefore very rich, since his action at each time t may depend on x_t. The utilities of both parties only depend on the final outcome x_1. That of the Agent is

$$u\left(x_1 - \int_0^1 a_t dt\right)$$

where u is the CARA[20] function

$$u(x) = -e^{-kx}$$

and the Principal is risk-neutral. The authors then show that the optimal contract is linear in x_1.

---

18. Robustness here refers to the ability to stay (at least approximately) optimal when the environment changes.

19. Recall that a Brownian motion is a set of random variables indexed by $t \in [0,1]$ such that each W_t follows a reduced centered normal $N(0, t)$ and increments are independent: If $t_1 < t_2 < t_3 < t_4$, $W_{t_2} - W_{t_1}$ and $W_{t_4} - W_{t_3}$ are independent. The Brownian motion is the statistical model for a continuous-time random walk.

20. CARA stands for constant absolute risk aversion.

One way to understand this result is to recall that the Brownian motion is the continuous-time limit of a discrete-time binomial process. Assume that the outcome may increase or decrease by a fixed amount in each period and that the Agent controls the probabilities of these two changes. As the utility function of the Agent is CARA and therefore exhibits no wealth effect, it can be shown that the optimal contract consists in repeating the contract that would be optimal in each period. But this contract gives a fixed wage to the Agent, plus a bonus if the outcome increased. The optimal contract for the whole period therefore must give the Agent a bonus that depends linearly on the number of periods in which the outcome increased. The result of Holmstrom-Milgrom clearly obtains by passing to the continuous-time limit.

This result in its strongest form relies on rather special assumptions; however, it does suggest that if the Principal only has an imperfect knowledge of the technology, the optimal contract may have a fairly simple form.

5.3.7 The Multitask Model

We assumed until now that all decisions taken by the Agent could be summed up in a single variable. This is of course unrealistic. Consider, for instance, an employee: His work typically consists of many distinct tasks, each of which requires effort and may generate a signal that is observed by the employer. When the Principal chooses a wage schedule, he must take into account this multiplicity of tasks. He must take care, for instance, not to reward the good accomplishment of one task to the point that it induces the Agent to forgo other tasks. Let us now look at a model that introduces such new trade-offs.

Assume that the Agent controls two effort variables a_1 and a_2. His utility function is given by

$$-\exp\left(-r(w - C(a_1, a_2))\right)$$

where r is a positive constant (the Agent's absolute risk aversion index) and C is a convex function. The Principal observes separately the profits he gets from each task:

$$\begin{cases} x_1 = a_1 + \varepsilon_1 \\ x_2 = a_2 + \varepsilon_2 \end{cases}$$

where the pair of observational noises $(\varepsilon_1, \varepsilon_2)$ follows a centered normal with variance

$$\Sigma = \begin{pmatrix} \sigma_1^2 & \sigma_{12} \\ \sigma_{12} & \sigma_2^2 \end{pmatrix}$$

The global profit of the Principal is the sum $(x_1 + x_2)$.

Given that we chose a CARA utility function for the Agent, we can use the results of Holmstrom-Milgrom (1987) presented in section 5.3.6 to limit our attention to linear wage contracts, that is,

$$w(x_1, x_2) = \alpha'x + \beta = \alpha_1 x_1 + \alpha_2 x_2 + \beta$$

With such a contract the Principal gets expected profits

$$a_1 + a_2 - \alpha_1 a_1 - \alpha_2 a_2 - \beta$$

while the Agent's expected utility has a certain equivalent[21]

$$\alpha_1 a_1 + \alpha_2 a_2 + \beta - C(a_1, a_2) - \frac{r}{2}\alpha' \Sigma \alpha$$

(I have used the formula that gives the expectation of an exponential function of a normal random variable X:

$$E \exp(-rX) = \exp\left(-rEX + \frac{r^2}{2}VX\right)$$

applied here to the random variable $\alpha'x$.)

---

21. Recall that for an agent whose von Neumann–Morgenstern utility function is u, the certain equivalent of a random wealth X is the number x such that $u(x) = Eu(X)$.

It appears from these formulæ that the parameter β only represents a transfer between the Principal and the Agent. The optimal contract thus is obtained by maximizing the expected total surplus

$$a_1 + a_2 - C(a_1, a_2) - \frac{r}{2} a' \Sigma a$$

under the incentive constraint that states that (a_1, a_2) maximizes

$$\alpha_1 a_1 + \alpha_2 a_2 - C(a_1, a_2)$$

Let us first study the consequences of the incentive constraint. It gives directly

$$\alpha_i = C_i'(a_1, a_2) \qquad (I)$$

By differentiating this, we obtain easily, for instance,

$$\begin{cases} \dfrac{\partial a_1}{\partial \alpha_1} = \dfrac{C_{22}''}{D''} \\[2mm] \dfrac{\partial a_1}{\partial \alpha_2} = -\dfrac{C_{12}''}{D''} \end{cases}$$

where D'' is the determinant of C'' and is positive. Therefore the Agent chooses an action a_1 that increases with α_1 and that decreases with α_2 if both tasks are substitutes $(C_{12}'' > 0)$. This simple remark is the key to the results to come.

Let us now come back to the optimal contract. By differentiating the expression for the expected total surplus with respect to a_i, we obtain

$$1 - C_i' - r\alpha' \Sigma \frac{\partial \alpha}{\partial a_i} = 0$$

whence, after differentiating (I),

$$\alpha = (I + rC'' \Sigma)^{-1} \begin{pmatrix} 1 \\ 1 \end{pmatrix}$$

Let us study some consequences of this formula. First assume that tasks are independent (C'' is diagonal) and that the signals are independent ($\sigma_{12} = 0$). Then we get

$$\alpha_i = \frac{1}{1 + rC''_{ii}\sigma_i^2}$$

the same formula as if the Principal had considered the two tasks separately.

Now let us come back to the more interesting case in which the matrix C'' may not be diagonal and assume that only the first task generates an observable signal. This can be modeled by letting $\sigma_{12} = 0$ and by making σ_2 go to infinity in the formula that gives α. In the limit one easily obtains $\alpha_2 = 0$ and

$$\alpha_1 = \frac{1 - (C''_{12}/C''_{22})}{1 + r\sigma_1^2\left[C''_{11} - ((C''_{12})^2/C''_{22})\right]} \qquad (G)$$

Taking as a benchmark the case of independent tasks, both the numerator and the denominator of the formula have changed. If, for instance, the two tasks are complements ($C''_{12} < 0$: an increase in a_1 makes a_2 less costly), α_1 will be higher when C''_{12} is more negative: The second task is not directly rewarded, since it does not generate an observable signal, but the corresponding incentives are carried over to the first task.

Under the same assumption that σ_2 is infinite, now assume that only total effort reduces the Agent's utility so that $C(a_1, a_2) = c(a_1 + a_2)$. Then not only $\alpha_2 = 0$, but since $C''_{11} = C''_{12} = C''_{22}$, formula (G) also yields $\alpha_1 = 0$. In this limit case in which the two tasks are perfect substitutes and one of them is nonobservable, inducing the Agent to perform in one task effectively discourages him to perform in the other. This dilemma brings the Principal to the point where he totally gives up on incentives.

Holmstrom-Milgrom (1991) rely on this last result to suggest that the multitask model may explain why real-life incentive schedules are less *high-powered*[22] than they are in our theoretical models: The fact that many tasks compete for the Agent's effort may induce the Principal to reduce the power of the incentives he provides to the Agent.

5.4   Examples of Applications

5.4.1   Insurance

The problem of insurance is the archetype of the conflict between risk-sharing and incentives that is at the basis of moral hazard. Risk-sharing indeed is the essential mission of insurance companies: By pooling risks, they rely on the law of large numbers to take responsibility for individual risks that (approximately) cancel out through aggregation. On the other hand, the magnitude of the risk itself depends on the behavior of the insurees: A cautious driver has fewer accidents. This creates an incentive problem that limits how much risk the insurer will be willing to bear, since it will be necessary to transfer some responsibility to the insurees by letting them bear some of the risk.

Consider, for instance, a driver who buys car insurance from an insurance company. Contrary to chapter 2, we will assume here that the driver's characteristics are completely known to the insurer. I will use the same notation as in chapter 2: The initial wealth of the driver is W, an accident costs him d, the premium is q, and the reimbursement R.

I will assume that the probability of an accident is a decreasing convex function $p(a)$ of the Agent's effort a;[23] a can be chosen in $[\underline{a}, \bar{a}]$. The cost of an effort a is just a, so the expected utility of the driver is

$$p(a)u(W - d + R - q) + (1 - p(a))u(W - q) - a$$

---

22. As mentioned in section 5.1, a schedule is high powered when it makes wages depend strongly on performance.

23. The literature sometimes makes a distinction between self-protection efforts, which reduce the probability of an accident, and self-insurance efforts, which reduce the size of the damage. Here I am focusing on self-protection.

while the expected profit of the (risk-neutral) insurance company is

$$q - p(a)R$$

The driver chooses his effort by maximizing his objective over a; in this simple model in which only two outcomes are possible, it is easy to check that p being decreasing implies MLRC and that its convexity implies CDFC, so we can apply the first-order approach. The Agent's choice thus is given by

$$p'(a)(u(W - d + R - q) - u(W - q)) = 1$$

If the reimbursement R was at least equal to the size of the damage d, the driver would choose the minimum self-protection effort $\underline{a}$, which is usually suboptimal. To induce the driver to be cautious, he must get a reimbursement lower than the size of the damage. This property is called *coinsurance*: In case of an accident its costs are shared between the insurance company (who pays R) and the driver (who suffers a loss $(d - R)$).

It would be easy to pursue the computations so as to solve the problem completely; the participation constraint

$$p(a)u(W - d + R - q) + (1 - p(a))u(W - q) - a = \underline{U}$$

indeed gives a second equation that allows us to write utilities as functions of a:

$$\begin{cases} u(W - d + R - q) = \underline{U} + a + \dfrac{1 - p(a)}{p'(a)} \\ u(W - q) = \underline{U} + a - \dfrac{p(a)}{p'(a)} \end{cases}$$

and therefore to write the premium and the reimbursement as functions of a, say, $q(a)$ and $R(a)$. All that remains to do is to maximize the Principal's objective

$$q(a) - p(a)R(a)$$

over a.

5.4.2   Wage Determination

Firms are prominent among economic organizations that worry about providing adequate incentives to their members. The study of how they do it therefore is both a natural application and an empirical test of the theories presented in this chapter. Obviously other sciences such as the sociology of organizations and psychology have much to say in this field; still the objective of the economist must be to push economic analysis as far as possible, by adopting the cynical viewpoint of the father of scientific management:

Hardly a competent worker can be found who does not devote a considerable amount of time to studying just how slowly he can work and still persuade his employer that he is going at a good pace. (Frederick Taylor, *The Principles of Scientific Management.*)

Baker-Jensen-Murphy (1988) give a critical survey of the difficulties that the theory faces in explaining how firms determine compensation. The book by Milgrom-Roberts (1992) also contains many enlightening discussions of both worker pay and managerial compensation.

Theory tells us that the best way to give incentives to employees is to identify one or several outcomes that constitute objective public signals of their effort and to condition their compensation on these outcomes. A caricatural form of such wage schedules is piece-rate wage, in which the employee is paid a function of the number of pieces he produces. This type of wage is only applicable in limited cases. Moreover it may be counterproductive if, for instance, the employee is lead to focus on the quantity he produces (which influences his wage) rather than on the quality of his work (which does not). It also tends to discourage cooperation among employees. In general, the employer must therefore try to identify a vector of outcomes that is as complete as possible. If he cannot do this, he will have to rely on subjective evaluations of the Agent's work, whose use is much more delicate and which may have perverse effects by inducing employees to spend much of their time lobbying their supervisors.

If individual evaluation is not practical, the employer may resort to collective evaluations. The simplest form of this is to use the firm's profit as an "outcome" and to condition wages on it. As for all collective evaluations, it raises the free-rider problem. Also it makes employees bear a risk that they may find difficult to diversify. It still is a rather popular solution, in part for macroeconomic or social reasons. Note that the use of franchises, in which a firm sells dealers the right to carry its brand, is an extreme example; in that case the Agent pays for the right to keep all profits, as he should in the first-best contract if he is risk-neutral.

Tournaments and the other relative performance evaluation procedures studied in section section 5.3.5 could be used, in principle, to determine wages among employees. In fact the empirical evidence is not very convincing on that point. On the other hand, this formula is very generally used (at least implicitly) to decide on promotions within the firm and thus to attribute the corresponding wage increases. Indeed observers have long noted that the dispersion of wages within a firm is extremely concentrated on changes in job level: Employees at a given level and with given seniority in that level have comparable wages,[24] but a change in job level is associated with a substantial wage increase. Thus promotions may well be the most important source of incentives in a firm.

The crudest way of inducing employees to work clearly is to threaten them with dismissal. This may be the only incentives available if outcomes from effort are observable but, for whatever reason, are not verifiable and thus may not condition an Agent's wage. However, threatening to fire employees who do not give satisfaction may be useless if unemployment is low, so that an employee who is dismissed may easily find a similar job at an equivalent wage. This idea lies at the basis of the famous Shapiro-Stiglitz (1984) model of involuntary unemployment. In this model employees will choose to shirk if their utility from working does not exceed that of being

---

24. This is often called "horizontal equity."

unemployed. To induce them to put on effort, the wage will have to be set higher than the market-clearing wage. This efficiency-wage model is at the heart of many neo-Keynesian explanations of involuntary unemployment.[25] In the same vein Lazear (1979) suggests that the reason we observe that wages increase with seniority is that this allows the firm to raise the cost of a dismissal for the employees and thus to increase their incentives to work. However, this explanation is only valid if firms want to keep their reputation for being fair employers, and thus they do not fire older employees whose wages are higher than their marginal productivity.

Managerial compensation raises specific problems. Managers are the relays of shareholders and take in their name decisions that govern the strategy of the firm. Inducing them to work is generally not considered to be a problem. On the other hand, they may have their own agenda in running the firm (maximizing perks or firm size, launching unprofitable but prestigious investments, etc.) Thus if they are to take decisions that increase the value of the firm, their interests should be aligned with those of the shareholders. There are some external devices to discipline managers, most notably their labor market and the threat of hostile takeovers; we are more concerned here with internal incentives. The easiest way to provide these incentives to managers would of course be to link their compensation to the value of the firm by paying them with shares. Neglecting managers' risk-aversion for the moment, this is a good solution so long as the value of the shares faithfully reflects the value of the firm; however, there can be doubts about that when the managers are in a strategic position to manipulate the value of the shares for their own benefit. One may also index managerial wages on profits, but this may induce managers to manipulate the firm's accounts or to take a short-term view. Finally, managers are often com-

---

25. On a more technical side, Shapiro-Stiglitz's model is interesting in that it uses labor demand to endogenize the participation constraint.

pensated by receiving stock options on the firm's share with a strike price that is slightly higher than the current price of the share. Such options allow the shareholders to reward managers who increase the value of the firm; however, they lose all incentive value if a negative shock badly affects the value of the firm.

Beyond these theoretical considerations, empirical studies show that managerial compensation is surprisingly low powered. Jensen-Murphy (1990) thus estimate that when the value of a large firm increases by $1,000, the discounted value of the total compensation[26] of its chief executive officer only increases by about $3. The survey by Rosen (1992) presents alternative estimates from which it can be concluded that even if the CEO manages to increase the stockmarket return of his firm's shares by ten percentage points (a fairly large change), his total compensation may not increase by more than a few percentage points. Given anecdotal evidence about how much a good or bad manager can affect his firm's profits, these figures seem very low. They could be justified by assuming that managers are very risk-averse, but this is clearly not an appealing explanation. The results on the multitask model presented in section 5.3.7 are probably more helpful here, since a CEO typically has many tasks to perform. It must be admitted, however, that these estimates present a puzzle for the theory.

Another interesting question is whether making a manager's pay performance-related increases his firm's performance. Evidence here is much more scarce. It appears that a firm's shares rise when it announces a long-term incentives plan. Moreover Abowd (1990) finds that higher bonus rates in year n increase the firm's market value in year $(n + 1)$. The available evidence thus suggests that performance-related managerial compensation does work. This makes it all the more surprising that there seems to be so little of it.

---

26. This includes the effect not only of bonus, shares, and options but also of the probability that the manager is fired. Thus this is a *maximum maximorum* estimate.

Exercises

Exercise 5.1

Go back to the two-action, two-outcome model of section 5.1. We want to prove that if $W_1 > W_0$, the Principal's utility is greater when the Agent succeeds than when he fails.

1. Using the definitions of w_S, w_F, and w and Jensen's inequality,[27] show that $pw_S + (1 - p)w_F > w$.

2. Going back to the expression for $W_1 - W_0$ in the text, show that if $x_S - w_S \leq x_F - w_F$, then $W_1 < W_0$.

3. State your conclusions.

Exercise 5.2

In the standard model, show that first-order stochastic dominance implies MLRC if there are only two possible outcomes.

Exercise 5.3

This exercise shows why the Principal's expected profit may decrease when the Agent becomes more productive, even in the two-by-two model of section 5.1. Start from values of the primitives such that $W_1 > W_0$.

1. Write W_1 as a function of p and P, and show that

$$\frac{\partial W_1}{\partial p} = -\frac{P(1 - P)}{(P - p)^2} \left(\frac{1}{u'(w_S)} - \frac{1}{u'(w_F)} \right) < 0$$

---

27. Recall that Jensen's inequality states that if X is a random variable and f is a convex function, then

$Ef(X) \geq f(EX)$.

2. Conclude that if the Agent gets more productive so that both p and P increase, it may be that W_1 decreases.

References

Abowd, J. 1990. Does performance-based managerial compensation affect corporate performance? *Industrial and Labor Relations Review* 43:52S–73S.

Baker, G., M. Jensen, and K. Murphy. 1988. Compensation and incentives: Practice vs. theory. *Journal of Finance* 43:593–616.

Gjesdal, F. 1982. Information and incentives: The Agency information problem. *Review of Economic Studies* 49:373–90.

Green, J., and N. Stokey. 1983. A comparison of tournaments and contracts. *Journal of Political Economy* 91:349–64.

Grossman, S., and O. Hart. 1983. An analysis of the principal-agent problem. *Econometrica* 51:7–45.

Holmstrom, B. 1979. Moral hazard and observability. *Bell Journal of Economics* 10:74–91.

Holmstrom, B. 1982. Moral hazard in teams. *Bell Journal of Economics* 13:324–40.

Holmstrom, B., and P. Milgrom. 1987. Aggregation and linearity in the provision of intertemporal incentives. *Econometrica* 55:303–28.

Holmstrom, B., and P. Milgrom. 1991. Multitask principal-agent analyses: Incentive contracts, asset ownership and job design. *Journal of Law, Economics and Organization* 7:24–51.

Itoh, H. 1991. Incentives to help in multi-agent situations. *Econometrica* 59:611–36.

Jensen, M., and K. Murphy. 1990. Performance pay and top-management incentives. *Journal of Political Economy* 98:225–64.

Jewitt, I. 1988. Justifying the first-order approach to principal-agent problems. *Econometrica* 56:1177–90.

Kim, S. K. 1995. Efficiency of an information system in an agency model. *Econometrica* 63:89–102.

Lazear, E. 1979. Why is there mandatory retirement? *Journal of Political Economy* 87:1261–84.

Milgrom, P., and J. Roberts. 1992. *Economics, Organization and Management*. Englewood Cliffs, NJ: Prentice Hall.

Mookherjee, D. 1984. Optimal incentive schemes in multi-agent situations. *Review of Economic Studies* 51:433–46.

Page, F. 1987. The existence of optimal contracts in the principal-agent model. *Journal of Mathematical Economics* 16:157-67.

Rogerson, W. 1985. The first-order approach to principal-agent problems. *Econometrica* 53:1357–68.

Rosen, S. 1992. Contracts and the market for executives. In *Contract Economics*, L. Werin and H. Wijkander, eds. Oxford: Basil Blackwell.

Shapiro, C., and J. Stiglitz. 1984. Equilibrium unemployment as a worker discipline device. *American Economic Review* 74:433–44.

6

The Dynamics of Complete Contracts

I only considered so far very elementary forms of economic relationships: a contract was signed, then all parties took decisions based on their preferences and on the terms of the contract, and then they separated. Real-life economic relationships obviously are much more complex, if only because their actors face each other for more or less extended time periods. The recognition that contracts have a time dimension has spawned a very abundant literature in recent years; this chapter and the next one aim at presenting its most general conclusions.

I will first present the key concepts of commitment and renegotiation that lie at the heart of the dynamic theory of contracts. Then I will study in this chapter the case where the contracts that are signed take into account all variables that are or may become relevant: The contracts are then said to be *complete*.

The dynamics of complete contracts today is fairly well understood, so I will offer a reasonably wide perspective.[1] Such is not the case for the more recent theory of *incomplete* contracts, which I will survey in chapter 7.

---

1. However, the proofs of the main results are often very complex, so I will sometimes only give the underlying intuition.

6.1   Commitment and Renegotiation

I have already underlined the importance of institutions in the theory of contracts. Introducing the time dimension and dynamic aspects gives a new weight to two key notions: commitment and renegotiation.

Commitment refers to the ability of agents to restrict their future actions in advance by pledging that they will stick to the contract until some predetermined date. The duration of commitment thus determines how rigid the contract is. The ability to commit depends on a number of factors:

• The institutional setup, as embodied in contractual law.

• The credibility of agents, through the importance they attach to their reputation, for instance.

• The existence of "hostages," which are assets or property titles that lose most of their value outside of the relationship under study. For instance, the computer manufacturer Apple built very specific factories when it launched the Macintosh. This investment was meant to persuade Apple's competitors and customers that the firm was determined to support its new product.

• The penalties specified in the contract in case one of the parties unilaterally decides to break it.

Breach of contract and renegotiation are the opposite of commitment. A breach of contract is a unilateral decision: One of the parties takes note that the contract does not serve its interests any more and decides to disengage itself. In this case it will incur the penalties determined by law or in the contract. These penalties may not exist; thus any employee can break his contract at any time (sometimes by giving advance notice), and his employer is not entitled to any compensation. We speak of renegotiation, on the other hand, when all parties agree to replace the existing contract with a new contract.

Renegotiation is multilateral by definition, and thus no party may claim any penalty.

I will distinguish in the following four degrees of commitment:[2]

• I will speak of *spot commitment* or *no commitment* when the contract only holds for the current period.[3] Once the parties reach the end of this period, they can only continue collaborating if they sign a new contract.

• At the opposite, I will speak of *full commitment* when the contract that is signed covers the whole duration of the relationship and it cannot be breached or renegotiated. Such a contract is never reconsidered, and the dynamic aspects of the contractual relationship reduce to the execution of the contract.

• There is *long-term commitment with renegotiation* (or simply *long-term commitment*) if the contract covers the whole duration of the relationship but it can be renegotiated multilaterally. Thus the contract can only be reconsidered if all parties agree to do so.

• Finally, I will speak of *short-term commitment*[4] or *limited commitment* in all intermediate cases between spot commitment and long-term commitment. These contracts then do not last as long as the relationship and may be renegotiated.

The kind of contracts that can be signed directly depends on what degree of commitment is assumed to hold. With no commitment, parties can only sign so-called "spot" contracts which only govern the current period. With full or long-term commitment, they can resort to long-term contracts that govern the whole relationship. Finally, I will call short-term contracts the contracts that can be

---

2. The terminology is not completely standard in this field; thus the terms I use should be used with caution.

3. The exact definition of a "period" depends on the context.

4. *Caveat lector*: The use of the "short-term" adjective may be slightly confusing; some authors do not distinguish between spot commitment and short-term commitment. However, I think this distinction is important.

signed when commitment is limited; these contracts cover a fraction of the duration of the relationship.

A fundamental result of the theory of individual choices is that no agent, taken in isolation, may gain by limiting his freedom of choice. Such is not the case any more when several agents interact. The famous prisoner dilemma is a striking example: Both players here have two strategies, since they can cooperate or defect. The only Nash equilibrium has both players defecting, and it is Pareto-dominated by the outcome in which both players cooperate. If the players could commit to cooperate (thus forbidding themselves to use the "defect" strategy), they would both reach a higher utility level.

It is easy to see that if contracts are complete, full commitment must be beneficial. Assume indeed that commitment is less than full and that the interaction ends up with some outcome A. If full commitment is available, the agents could then just commit to achieve outcome A; thus any outcome that is feasible without full commitment can be achieved with full commitment. The agents cannot lose, and may even win, if they choose to "burn their boats."[5] We will see, however, in chapter 7 that commitment is less valuable when contracts are incomplete. In that case some variables that influence the parameters of the relationship under study have not been integrated in the contract in advance; renegotiation may then allow the parties to take them into account and thus to improve the efficiency of the contractual relationship.

6.2 Strategic Commitment

Before I turn to the dynamics of complete contracts, I want to survey briefly here the literature on *strategic commitment*. The central theme of this field is that signing a contract can have *precommitment effects* on a third party by convincing it that the contractants will persist in

---

5. Cortez is said to have burnt his ships on arriving in Mexico so as to convince his troops and the indigenous populations of his determination.

their plans whatever it does. Thus it offers another illustration of the importance of commitment in contracting.

The idea of strategic commitment goes back to Schelling (1960). Early papers that formalized his intuitions included the work of Brander-Spencer (1985), who showed that export subsidies may improve welfare in the home country and of Fershtman-Judd (1987), who studied the strategic use of managerial incentives in a Cournot oligopoly.

I will present here in some detail the paper by Aghion-Bolton (1987), which introduced a new way for a firm to prevent entry on its market. This has long been a central theme of industrial organization. Several contractual devices can be used in that purpose in manufacturer-retailer relationships, for instance, *exclusive dealing*, which forbids a retailer for one brand to also sell a competing brand. The legality of such practices depends on prevailing statutes, and even more crucially on the way they are applied. Authors belonging to the Chicago school[6] consider that such contracts should not be illegal, since buyers would not accept to sign them if they were detrimental to their utility. We will see here that even though this argument is basically right, exclusive contracts may still reduce competition and create social inefficiencies.

Consider a seller S who produces a good at cost $1/2$. This seller proposes the good to a unique buyer B who only buys zero or one unit of the good and whose reservation price is 1. A potential entrant E produces the same good at cost c. Neither B nor S know the exact value of c; they just have a prior which we take to be the uniform distribution on $[0, 1]$, so the entrant may or may not be more efficient than the seller.

We assume that if E does enter the market, he and S will compete in prices à la Bertrand; the equilibrium price then is the highest of the two production costs, or

---

6. The Chicago school is associated with a rather lax attitude as far as competition policy is concerned.

$$P = \max\left(\frac{1}{2}, c\right)$$

If there is no contract between S and B, E will enter if and only if his cost is smaller than $1/2$, which has probability $\varphi = 1/2$. The price will be 1 if E does not enter and $1/2$ if he does. Thus the buyer has expected surplus $1/4$, and so does S.

Now assume that B and S can sign a contract (chosen and proposed by S) before E decides whether he should enter. Also assume that c is not observed by B or S ex post, so the contract cannot be contingent on the value of c. It is easy to show that the optimal contract must be a pair (P, P_0), where P is the price B must pay to S if he buys the good from him and P_0 is the penalty he must pay to S if he decides to buy from E instead.

Under these circumstances B will buy from E only if the latter sets a price lower than $(P - P_0)$, and E will choose a price equal to $(P - P_0)$ if he enters the market.[7] E will thus only enter if his cost c is lower than $(P - P_0)$, and the probability of entry becomes

$$\varphi' = \max(0, P - P_0) \qquad (P)$$

which depends on the terms of the contract. Finally, the buyer will not sign such a contract unless it gives him at least as much expected surplus as no contract,[8] that is, $1/4$. Since the buyer's surplus is $(1 - P)$ if he buys from S and the entrant optimally should not give him a higher surplus, we must have

$$1 - P \geq \frac{1}{4} \qquad (IR)$$

Now compute S's expected surplus. It is $(P - 1/2)$ if E does not enter and P_0 if E enters the market (in which case the buyer buys from him). The optimal contract (P, P_0) therefore must maximize

---

7. We assume here that if B is indifferent between both sellers, he chooses to buy from E.

8. This is the Chicago school argument mentioned earlier.

$$\varphi'P_0 + (1 - \varphi')\left(P - \frac{1}{2}\right)$$

under both constraints (P) and (IR).

First consider the possibility that $P < P_0$. In that case $\varphi' = 0$, and the objective is $(P - 1/2)$, which, given (IR), is maximal in $P = 3/4$, where it is $1/4$. Now, if $P \geq P_0$, $\varphi' = P - P_0$; canceling the derivative of the objective with respect to P_0 gives $P_0 = P - 1/4$ and reinjecting it into the objective shows that it becomes $P - 7/16$, which, given (IR), is maximal in $P = 3/4$ again but equals $5/16$, which is greater than $1/4$. Thus the optimum is given by $(P, P_0) = (3/4, 1/2)$.

At the optimum, B gets the same surplus as without a contract, since $1 - 3/4 = 1/4$. On the other hand, the contract allows S to get a higher surplus, since that increases from $1/4$ to $5/16$. Finally, the probability of entry now is $1/4$; in particular, when $1/4 < c < 1/2$, E does not enter, and the less efficient seller produces the good: There is *market foreclosure*.

Thus signing a contract with B that punishes B when he buys from the entrant allows S to reduce the competitive pressure on his profits. Even though this contract does not hurt the buyer, it takes the producers away from the production optimum in which the buyer buys from S when $c > 1/2$ and from E when $c < 1/2$. This model thus suggests that this type of contractual practice should be forbidden.

In this example, a party (the seller) tries to deter another party (the entrant) from taking a certain decision (here entering the market) by signing a contract with a third party (the buyer) and making it public. This behavior, based on precommitment effects, is the essence of strategic commitment. Katz (1991) has a similar, perfect information model in which a seller who values a good at 1 faces a buyer who values it at 2. If the seller sets the price, he will appropriate all the surplus by pricing the good at 2. However, if the buyer signs a public contract with an intermediary, promising to buy the good only from him and at price 1, then the equilibrium price will be 1 and the buyer will appropriate all the surplus. Clearly one problem with both the Aghion-Bolton and Katz models is that the public contracts are not robust to renegotiation: In Katz's model, if the seller decides to price the good at 1.5 after all, the buyer and the intermediary will want to renegotiate their contract. Dewatripont (1988) shows that one must introduce asymmetric information at the renegotiation stage if such contracts are to survive renegotiation. Caillaud-Jullien-Picard (1995) is a more recent paper that studies two competing Principal-Agent structures that can sign public contracts and then secretly renegotiate them; it shows that more competitive outcomes (which benefit customers and hurt the competing structures) may actually emerge as a result.

6.3 What Are Complete Contracts?

I will begin my study of dynamic aspects of the theory of contracts by analyzing the case in which contracts are complete. This should be taken to mean that all variables that may have an impact on the conditions of the contractual relationship during its whole duration have been taken into account when negotiating and signing the contract. Thus the contract may be contingent on a very large number of variables. This assumption implies that no unforeseen contingency may arise as the relationship evolves: Any change in the economic environment just activates the ad hoc provisions of the contract.

As we saw in section 6.1, full commitment is beneficial when contracts are complete. Therefore the study of the dynamics of complete contracts essentially consists in tracking when and why other forms of commitment involve efficiency losses.

I will first analyze a reasonably general adverse selection model; then I will turn to repeated moral hazard models.

6.4   Adverse Selection

I will consider in this section an intertemporal price discrimination model that possesses all features of general repeated adverse selection models.[9]

The model has T periods. In each period t the Principal produces at unit cost c a perishable good in quantity q and sells it to a consumer for a price p. The utilities of both parties are

$$\sum_{t=1}^{T} \delta^{t-1}(p_t - cq_t)$$

for the Principal and

$$\sum_{t=1}^{T} \delta^{t-1}(u(q_t)\theta - p_t)$$

for the Agent who is a type θ consumer. The consumer may be of type $\underline{\theta}$ or $\overline{\theta}$, with $\overline{\theta} > \underline{\theta} > 0$. The proportion of types $\underline{\theta}$ in the population is π. The parameter θ, which is only observed by the Agent, therefore represents the consumer's valuation for the good; it is assumed to be constant over time.[10] I will assume that u is increasing and concave, and that

$$u(0) = 0, \ u'(0) = \infty \text{ and } u'(\infty) = 0$$

which implies, inter alia, the Spence-Mirrlees condition.

The first-best optimal consumptions are obtained by solving the program

$$\max_{q} (u(q)\theta - cq)$$

---

9. For all of this section, the reader may turn to the fourth part of the Laffont-Tirole (1993) book, which studies in detail a somewhat different model but reaches very similar conclusions.

10. See Baron-Besanko (1984) for a model in which θ changes over time.

whence

$$\theta u'(q) = c$$

I will denote them by $\underline{q}^*$ and $\bar{q}^*$ in the following. Of course $\underline{q}^* < \bar{q}^*$.

First consider the one-period model ($T = 1$). Let $(\underline{q}, \underline{p}, \bar{q}, \bar{p})$ be the second-best optimal direct truthful mechanism. The general results I established in chapter 2 apply to this model. It follows that the consumption of type $\bar{\theta}$ is $\bar{q} = \bar{q}^*$, that the incentive constraint

$$u(\bar{q})\bar{\theta} - \bar{p} = u(\underline{q})\bar{\theta} - \underline{p}$$

is binding, and that type $\underline{\theta}$ gets his reservation utility level:

$$u(\underline{q})\underline{\theta} - \underline{p} = 0$$

Therefore $\underline{q}$ is given by maximizing the Principal's objective:

$$\max_{\underline{q}} \left(\pi(u(\underline{q})\underline{\theta} - c\underline{q}) + (1 - \pi)(u(\bar{q}^*)\bar{\theta} - u(\underline{q})\bar{\theta} + u(\underline{q})\underline{\theta} - c\bar{q}^*) \right)$$

whence

$$u'(\underline{q})(\underline{\theta} - (1 - \pi)\bar{\theta}) = \pi c$$

I will assume[11] that $\underline{\theta} > (1 - \pi)\bar{\theta}$. The low-type consumption $\underline{q}$ then is a positive quantity that is lower than $\underline{q}^*$: As in chapter 2 the consumption of the lower type is underefficient.

6.4.1   Full Commitment

The revelation principle applies when commitment is full: The two parties indeed interact only once because the contract is never reconsidered, and thus the proof of the revelation principle given in chapter 2 holds without change. The Principal therefore must propose a direct mechanism $(\underline{q}_t, \bar{q}_t, \underline{p}_t, \bar{p}_t)_{t=1}^T$

• which is truthful,

---

11. Otherwise it would be optimal for the Principal to exclude the low type, as discussed in chapter 2.

$$\left\{ \begin{array}{l} \displaystyle\sum_{t=1}^{T} \delta^{t-1}(u(\underline{q}_t)\underline{\theta} - \underline{p}_t) \geq \sum_{t=1}^{T} \delta^{t-1}(u(\overline{q}_t)\underline{\theta} - \overline{p}_t) \\[3mm] \displaystyle\sum_{t=1}^{T} \delta^{t-1}(u(\overline{q}_t)\overline{\theta} - \overline{p}_t) \geq \sum_{t=1}^{T} \delta^{t-1}(u(\underline{q}_t)\overline{\theta} - \underline{p}_t) \end{array} \right.$$

- and which satisfies both intertemporal individual rationality constraints,

$$\left\{ \begin{array}{l} \displaystyle\sum_{t=1}^{T} \delta^{t-1}(u(\underline{q}_t)\underline{\theta} - \underline{p}_t) \geq 0 \\[3mm] \displaystyle\sum_{t=1}^{T} \delta^{t-1}(u(\overline{q}_t)\overline{\theta} - \overline{p}_t) \geq 0 \end{array} \right.$$

Let $M_1^T = (\underline{q}_t, \overline{q}_t, \underline{p}_t, \overline{p}_t)_{t=1}^{T}$ be the optimal mechanism, and consider, in the one-period model, the stochastic mechanism M that consists in giving the Agent the following lottery:

$$\left\{ \begin{array}{lll} (\underline{q}_1, \overline{q}_1, \underline{p}_1, \overline{p}_1) & \text{with probability} & \dfrac{1}{1 + \delta + \ldots + \delta^{T-1}} \\[3mm] \ldots & \ldots & \ldots \\[3mm] (\underline{q}_T, \overline{q}_T, \underline{p}_T, \overline{p}_T) & \text{with probability} & \dfrac{\delta^{T-1}}{1 + \delta + \ldots + \delta^{T-1}} \end{array} \right.$$

It is easy to check that just as mechanism M_1^T in the T-period model, the stochastic mechanism M is truthful and satisfies the individual rationality constraints in the one-period model. Thus it cannot give the Principal more utility than the optimal mechanism in the one-period model, so

$$\frac{1}{1 + \delta + \ldots + \delta^{T-1}} \sum_{t=1}^{T} \delta^{t-1}\Big(\pi(\underline{p}_t - c\underline{q}_t) + (1 - \pi)(\overline{p}_t - c\overline{q}_t)\Big)$$
$$\leq \pi(\underline{p} - c\underline{q}) + (1 - \pi)(\overline{p} - c\overline{q})$$

whence, in the T-period model this time,

$$\sum_{t=1}^{T} \delta^{t-1}\Big(\pi(\underline{p}_t - c\underline{q}_t) + (1 - \pi)(\bar{p}_t - c\bar{q}_t)\Big)$$

$$\leq \sum_{t=1}^{T} \delta^{t-1}\Big(\pi(\underline{p} - c\underline{q}) + (1 - \pi)(\bar{p} - c\bar{q})\Big)$$

This argument proves that when commitment is full, the optimal mechanism consists in proposing for each period the so-called static optimum of the one-period model.

This result is intuitive: With full commitment the Principal must propose a contract that binds the parties for the T periods. In such a stationary model there is no reason to give an allocation that is not itself stationary.

The properties of the full commitment optimum are summed up in figure 6.1, which illustrates the sequence of consumptions q that each type of Agent gets in each period in a two-period model.

The Agent of type $\bar{\theta}$ takes the upper branch in figure 6.1, and the Agent of type $\underline{\theta}$ takes the lower branch. Thus types separate in the first period.

6.4.2 Long-Term Commitment

Now assume that the Principal and the Agent can renegotiate the full commitment optimal contract $(\underline{q}, \bar{q}, \underline{p}, \bar{p})_{t=1}^{T}$. Consider, for instance,

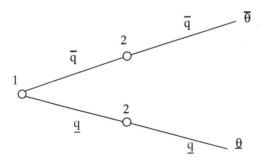

Figure 6.1
The full commitment optimum

the beginning of the second period. Since the contract is separating in the first period, the Principal then knows the type of the Agent. If the Agent has type $\underline{\theta}$, the full commitment optimum has him consume the underefficient quantity $\underline{q}$ until the end of the relationship: To reach the highest level of efficiency ex ante (before the relationship starts and in expectation over types), we had to accept that contractual allocations be inefficient ex post (once the execution of the contract has started). This property is often summed up by saying that the parties commit ex ante to ex post inefficient allocations.

The Principal and the type $\underline{\theta}$ Agent would be better off by signing at the beginning of the second period a new contract under which the Agent consumes the efficient quantity q^* in each period $t = 2$, ..., T. The full commitment optimal contract therefore cannot be an equilibrium in a long-term commitment situation: We say that it is not robust to renegotiation. This property means that such a contract may not be a very useful descriptive tool. It is indeed difficult to imagine a mechanism that would allow the parties to commit ex ante never to renegotiate the contract. There is nothing in contractual law to prevent the parties from renegotiating the contract by common agreement. They might of course stipulate in the contract that they should both pay a penalty to a third party if they choose to renegotiate, but they would then gain ex post by bribing the third party so that it does not enact the proposed penalty. This would increase their utilities and that of the third party, since the latter does not get any penalty in equilibrium anyway. Thus full commitment can only be a relevant concept if the costs of renegotiating are high enough or if the parties try to maintain a reputation for inflexibility, but both of these cases are outside of our model.

Recent research has therefore aimed at realism by concentrating on the long-term commitment concept introduced by Dewatripont (1989). It is easy to show that at the optimum when renegotiation is allowed, there will actually be no renegotiation, since any future renegotiation can be anticipated and built into the long-term contract; this is sometimes called the *renegotiation-proofness principle*.

The long-term commitment optimal contract covers periods 1 to T and is such that at no point in time its continuation can be replaced by a renegotiation-proof contract that gives more utility to the Principal and at least as much utility to the Agent on the remaining periods. To the usual incentive and individual rationality constraints, one must therefore add nonrenegotiation constraints at each period. These new constraints can also be interpreted as *sequential efficiency* constraints, since they ensure that the contract must be ex post efficient. They make the computation of the optimum very difficult. Therefore I will just describe its properties here, while directing the reader to Hart-Tirole (1988) or Laffont-Tirole (1990) for the proofs.

Renegotiation eliminates ex post inefficiencies through the sequential efficiency constraints. On the other hand, it creates ex ante inefficiencies, since the optimal mechanism must satisfy these new constraints. It must also involve a more progressive revelation of information than under the full commitment optimum. The ability to renegotiate indeed implies that the revelation principle does not apply any more, since the game becomes truly dynamic.

To describe the long-term commitment optimum, I will concentrate on the consumption paths followed by the different types of the Agent. It can be shown that at each period t, two consumption levels are possible: the efficient consumption for $\bar{\theta}$, that is, $\bar{q}^*$, and a lower consumption q_t. The consumption level $\bar{q}^*$ is only chosen by type $\bar{\theta}$; in fact, an Agent who chooses $\bar{q}^*$ in period t reveals that his type is $\bar{\theta}$ and must therefore consume $\bar{q}^*$ until the end of the relationship. On the other hand, consumption q_t is chosen by the $\underline{\theta}$ type and, with some probability, by the $\bar{\theta}$ type. In each period

- Agent $\underline{\theta}$ consumes q_t;

- Agent $\bar{\theta}$, if he has not chosen $\bar{q}^*$ yet, plays a mixed strategy in that he consumes q_t or $\bar{q}^*$, with probabilities fixed by the optimality conditions;

- Agent $\bar{\theta}$, if he has already consumed $\bar{q}^*$ in the past, keeps doing so.

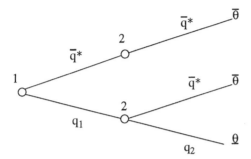

Figure 6.2
The long-term optimum

The long-term optimum therefore has a much more complex structure than the full commitment optimum: Agent $\bar{\theta}$ reveals his type in the first period with some probability; if he does not actually reveal it, then he can do so in the second period, and so on. The Principal only learns the type of the Agent once the latter has consumed $\bar{q}^*$, which he can do in any period.

Figure 6.2 illustrates the long-term optimum in a two-period model;[12] Agent $\bar{\theta}$ follows the two upper branches, and Agent $\underline{\theta}$ only follows the lowest branch. It is in fact fairly easy to compute q_2. Assume that in the first period the good type takes the upper branch with probability x. Then at the beginning of the second period and if the Agent consumed q_1 in the first period, the Principal will use Bayes's rule to revise his prior π to

$$\pi_2 = \frac{\pi}{\pi + (1 - \pi)(1 - x)}$$

He then faces an Agent who is a low type with probability π_2 and a high type with probability $(1 - \pi_2)$. Since this is the last period of the game, the solution is exactly the same as in the one-period problem,

12. The shape of the optimal contract in fact depends on the parameters of the model and especially on the prior probabilities; the configuration presented here is the most typical, however.

with the only difference that π is replaced with π_2: The Principal will give the Agent the choice between $\bar{q}^*$ and an underefficient consumption level q_2 designed for the low type and given by the by now familiar equation

$$u'(q_2)(\underline{\theta} - (1 - \pi_2)\bar{\theta}) = \pi_2 c$$

This characterizes the solution in the second period. Unfortunately, the determination of x and q_1 is more involved.

6.4.3   No Commitment

In the long-term commitment optimum, the Agent of type $\bar{\theta}$ gets a positive informational rent in each period, even after he has revealed his type. The Principal may therefore be tempted, once he sees the Agent consuming $\bar{q}^*$, to break the contract. He would then have perfect information: Since he faces an Agent whom he knows is of type $\bar{\theta}$, he could extract all of his surplus[13] by pricing the good at $p = u(\bar{q}^*)\bar{\theta}$ in each remaining period.

In the absence of commitment, any party can effectively break the contract at the end of each period. In particular, the Principal can immediately exploit any information that is revealed by the Agent. The latter will therefore be very reluctant to reveal information on his type. This is the celebrated *ratchet effect*: It is extremely costly for the Principal to get the Agent to reveal any information, since the Agent knows that by so doing, he will allow the Principal to reap all the surplus. To get the Agent $\bar{\theta}$ to reveal his type in, say, the first period, the Principal must therefore bribe him by giving him all his expected discounted informational rent in the first period, but by so doing, he risks inducing Agent $\underline{\theta}$ to pretend he is $\bar{\theta}$ so as to benefit from the bribe.[14] This dilemma leads the Principal to adopt revela-

---

13. That is, leave the Agent zero utility.
14. This stands in contrast with the one-period model, in which the only binding incentive constraint prevents $\bar{\theta}$ from mimicking $\underline{\theta}$.

tion schemes that are even more progressive than under long-term commitment.

Solving the Principal's problem with no commitment requires computing the perfect Bayesian equilibrium of the game in which

• in the first period the Principal proposes a nonlinear tariff $p_1(q_1)$ and the Agent chooses a consumption q_1;

• given the observed consumption q_1, the Principal updates his prior π, which becomes $\pi_2(q_1)$, then he offers in the second period a new nonlinear tariff $p_2(q_1, q_2)$, and so on.

The complete solution of this game is very complex.[15] Let me just point out that the importance of the ratchet effect crucially depends on the patience of both parties (summed up in δ) and on the duration T of the relationship. If δ and T are both small, then the Agent will not lose much discounted informational rent by revealing his information early; information revelation will be progressive but reasonably fast. On the other hand, if δ and T are large, then the Agent will only reveal his information very slowly (see Laffont-Tirole 1987).

6.4.4   Short-Term Commitment

I have regrouped under "short-term commitment" all degrees of commitment that are intermediate between no commitment and long-term commitment. Here contracts may still be renegotiated, but their duration is shorter than that of the relationship.

Rey-Salanié (1996) study the example of two-period contracts that are renegotiable at each date but cannot be broken unilaterally before they expire. They show that if price and quantity transfers are unlimited, these contracts implement the long-term optimum. To understand this result, consider the beginning of the first period; the

---

15. Freixas-Guesnerie-Tirole (1985) solve the game under the restriction that contracts are linear (the payment p is linear in q). This considerably simplifies the analysis, so their paper is a good place to start.

Principal then proposes a contract $C_1 = (p_1(q_1), \tilde{p}_2(q_1, q_2))$ that specifies the transfers that the Agent must pay to the Principal in the first two periods as functions of his consumptions. But since the contract can be renegotiated (and will be in equilibrium) at the beginning of the second period, the only part the "promise" $\tilde{p}_2(q_1, q_2)$ plays is to set up the conditions for the future renegotiation. The difficulty is to choose $\tilde{p}_2$ so that it gives every type of the Agent the right continuation utility. It can be shown that this can be done so that future renegotiations lead both parties to replicate the equilibrium path that leads to the long-term optimum.

6.4.5 Conclusion

To sum up this section:

• Full commitment leads to the most efficient contracts and brings immediate revelation of information; however, it is not very realistic, in general, since it implies that the parties commit to ex post inefficient allocations that are vulnerable to renegotiation.

• Long-term commitment induces a more progressive revelation of information and an ex ante efficiency loss.

• Under certain conditions short-term commitment implements the same allocations as long-term commitment.

• Finally, no commitment introduces the ratchet effect; information revelation may be very slow, and the allocations that obtain are less efficient than under all other forms of commitment.

6.5 Moral Hazard

The study of intertemporal moral hazard is much more complex than that of adverse selection models. There are two reasons for this:

• The wage that the Agent receives at period t depends on his effort and on a shock that he does not control; it is therefore a stochastic income for him. As any ordinary consumer who has a concave utility function and receives a random income stream, he will want to smooth his consumption, if he can, by saving and borrowing (or by running down his savings). The study of intertemporal moral hazard therefore cannot abstract from the conditions under which the Agent can access credit markets.

· The repetition of a moral hazard problem can create endogenously private information for the Agent. As we will see later, this will be the case if the technology or the preferences of the Agent in any given period depend on his actions in earlier periods. The dynamic moral hazard problem then is complicated by an intertemporal adverse selection problem similar to that we analyzed in section 6.4.

Before I present the characteristics of the repeated moral hazard problem, I will study a model due to Fudenberg-Tirole (1990) that shows that even one-period moral hazard problems have dynamic aspects.

6.5.1   Renegotiation after Effort

Let us return to the one-period model studied in chapter 5 and assume, for instance, that the technology is $x = a + \varepsilon$, where ε is an observational noise with mean zero. At the optimum the Principal announces a wage schedule $w^*(x)$, the Agent makes an effort a^* and expects to get a random wage given by $w^*(a^* + \varepsilon)$, while the Principal gets a surplus $(a^* + \varepsilon - w^*(a^* + \varepsilon))$.

We saw in chapter 5 that the shape taken by the function w^* results from a trade-off between incentives and risk-sharing. Let us now consider a point in time when the Agent has made effort a^* but the outcome x has not been observed yet. The function w^* then has played its part in providing incentives to the Agent, and only risk-sharing matters now. But if we assume as usual that the Principal is risk-neutral and the Agent is risk-averse, the risk-sharing properties of the function w^* cannot be optimal; the optimum would be a constant wage (independent of ε) so that the Principal insures the Agent perfectly against the risk represented by the shock ε.

This argument shows that once the Agent has made effort a^*, the parties would gain by renegotiating toward a perfect insurance contract that gives all risk to the Principal. The optimal contract therefore is not robust to renegotiation. Obviously, if the Agent anticipates that his wage schedule will be renegotiated to a constant wage after he chooses his effort, he will choose the least costly action: The contract w^* cannot play any incentive role any more, since the Agent knows that this contract will eventually be replaced with a constant wage.

The idea that the parties may renegotiate after the Agent has chosen his action is more or less natural according to the situation under study: It is, for instance, not very reasonable in an employer-employee relationship. On the other hand, it may have more weight when the time interval between the choice of action and the observation of the outcome is longer; think, for instance, of the construction of a bridge or a weapons system for the government.

If this type of renegotiation is possible, then it must be taken into account when designing the optimal contract. Assume, for instance, that the action can only take two values, $a = 0$ and $a = 1$. The argument given above shows that $a = 1$ cannot be implemented with probability one. The optimal contract must therefore incite the Agent to choose $a = 0$ with some nonzero probability. In general, it will not be optimal to implement $a = 0$ with probability one; the Agent therefore has a totally mixed strategy. At the renegotiation date the Principal faces two possible types of Agent: one who chose $a = 1$, and one who chose $a = 0$; he must therefore solve an adverse selection problem similar to that of the monopoly insurance model studied in section 3.1.3. He will offer two different wage schedules, one for each type of Agent; the analogy with the insurance model suggests, and it can be shown, that the wage schedule designed for the Agent who chose action $a = 0$ insures him perfectly.

The essential lesson from this model is that if the two parties may renegotiate after effort has been chosen, then the Principal cannot get the Agent to choose the optimal effort with probability one any more. As in the repeated adverse selection model, the ability to renegotiate brings an efficiency loss.

*6.5.2 Convergence to the First-Best

I insisted in chapter 5 on the similarities between the incentive problem that the Principal faces and the classical problem of statistical inference: The Principal tries to infer the action a from observing the outcome x. It therefore seems likely that a law of large numbers should apply: If the interaction between the Principal and the Agent is repeated indefinitely, the Principal will observe a large number of outcomes; he will be able to infer the action with great precision and to punish the Agent very strongly if the latter does not choose the optimal action. In the limit the Principal should be able to implement the first-best optimal action.

Rubinstein-Yaari (1983) show that this intuition is right when neither the Principal nor the Agent has a preference for the present. Assume the technology is given by

$$x_t = a + \varepsilon_t$$

within each period t, where the ε_t are independent and identically distributed noises with mean zero and a finite variance σ^2. Let a^* be the first-best optimal action. If the Agent chooses a^* in each period, then by the law of large numbers, the average

$$\frac{1}{t}\sum_{\tau=1}^{t}(x_\tau - a^*)$$

will go to zero almost surely as t goes to infinitely. To induce the Agent to choose action a^* in each period, the Principal can then punish the Agent if the absolute value of this average is greater than some positive threshold, indicating that the Agent has deviated relatively often. The difficult point is how to choose this threshold: It should go to zero as t goes to infinity in order to take advantage of the law of large numbers, but it should not vanish too fast; otherwise the Agent would be punished too often when he chooses a^*, which would not be good for risk-sharing.

The appropriate tool for this problem is the law of the iterated logarithm, which bounds the large deviations from the law of large numbers. Let λ be any real number greater than 1, and let

$$\delta_t = \frac{\left(\sum_{\tau=1}^{t} \varepsilon_\tau\right)/t}{\sqrt{2\lambda\sigma^2 \ln \ln t/t}}$$

Then the law of the iterated logarithm states that

$$\Pr\left(\lim_{t\to\infty} \sup \delta_t < 1\right) = 1$$

The policy consisting in choosing a $\lambda > 1$ and punishing the Agent at date t if

$$\left|\frac{1}{t}\sum_{\tau=1}^{t} x_\tau - a^*\right| > \sqrt{\frac{2\lambda\sigma^2 \ln \ln t}{t}}$$

thus implements the first-best action if the punishment is rough enough and the interaction is repeated indefinitely. Note that if the Agent does choose a^* in each period, then he will be punished with vanishing probability.

The trouble with this result is that it rests on two crucial assumptions:

- That the interaction is infinitely repeated.
- That both agents are extremely patient.

The rest of this section is devoted to models in which the interaction is repeated over a finite horizon. Then the argument developed above fails completely and the optimum is clearly second-best.

6.5.3   Finitely Repeated Moral Hazard

Assume that the interaction between the Principal and the Agent
lasts for T periods. The Principal's utility function is

$$\sum_{t=1}^{T} \delta^{t-1}(x_t - w_t)$$

while that of the Agent is

$$\sum_{t=1}^{T} \delta^{t-1}(u(c_t) - a_t)$$

where u is increasing and concave and c_t is the consumption of the
Agent at time t (it is important to distinguish wage and consumption if the Agent has access to a credit market). The common dis-
count parameter δ is positive.

I will make the important assumption that the outcome in period t
only depends on the action chosen in the same period. If, for instance, the outcome in period t also depended on the action a_{t-1},
which is only observed by the Agent, then the latter would have an
informational advantage on the Principal at the beginning of period t,
since he would have a finer knowledge of the period-t technology.
Elements of adverse selection that I don't want to deal with now
would then complicate the moral hazard problem.[16]

The following discussion is adapted from Chiappori-Macho-Rey-
Salanié (1994).

No Access to Credit
First assume that the Agent cannot save or borrow, so his consumption equals his wage within any period.[17] An immediate application
of the dynamic programming principle shows that full commitment
coincides with long-term commitment in this model: The Agent's

---

16. They will turn up anyway when the Agent has free access to credit markets.
17. This clearly is an extreme assumption; however, the analysis would be the same if
the Agent were liquidity constrained and this constraint were active at the optimum.

characteristics are fully known to the Principal when the contract is signed, and the Principal therefore can choose the optimal sequence of wage schedules without ever feeling the need to adapt it to the arrival of new information.

Since the Agent has a concave utility function, he will want to have a smooth consumption over time. If the outcome x_t is particularly high because a favorable shock took place in period t, the Principal therefore will have to spread this positive shock over several periods so as to smooth the Agent's consumption stream.[18] He will do this by increasing the wage he gives to the Agent in all future periods. Thus the wage given in any period t will have to depend not only on the current outcome x_t but also on the sequence of past outcomes. This property, which Rogerson (1985) called the *memory effect*, therefore is a simple consequence of the need for the Principal to smooth the Agent's consumption at the full commitment optimum.

In the absence of commitment the Principal cannot spread the effect of a shock on x_t over several periods: He cannot indeed commit to anything in period $(t + 1)$, and not in particular to giving the Agent a period-$(t + 1)$ wage that depends on x_t. Therefore the period-t wage can only depend on the current outcome x_t, and the optimal sequence of spot contracts is memoryless: This clearly involves an important efficiency loss. Finally, Rey-Salanié (1990) show that short-term commitment allows the Principal to smooth the Agent's consumption optimally and thus implements the full commitment optimum.

Note that the full commitment optimum has a somewhat counterfactual property: It constrains the Agent to saving less than he would like. To prove this, assume that $T = 2$, and denote

- w_i the first-period wage when the first-period outcome is x_i,

- w_{ij} the second-period wage when the first-period outcome is x_i and that for the second period is x_j,

---

18. Note that the Principal only cares about total discounted wages, not about their timing.

- a_i the action the Agent chooses in the second period when the first-period outcome is x_i,

- $p_j(a)$ the probability of outcome x_j in any period when the chosen action in that period is a.

The solution of the incentive problem determines the gross utility U_{ij} the Agent must receive in each state of the world,

$$u(w_i) + \delta u(w_{ij}) = U_{ij} \qquad (C_{ij})$$

On the other hand, the Principal must provide incentives at least cost, that is, by minimizing for all i the wage bill

$$w_i + \delta \sum_{j=1}^{m} p_j(a_i) w_{ij}$$

under the m constraints $(C_{ij})_{j=1,\ldots,m}$ when the first-period outcome is x_i. Let λ_j be the multiplier associated to C_{ij} in this program; maximizing the Lagrangian gives

$$\begin{cases} 1 = \sum_{j=1}^{m} \lambda_j u'(w_j) \\ p_j(a_i) = \lambda_j u'(w_{ij}) \end{cases}$$

and the first-order condition for this problem therefore is[19]

$$\frac{1}{u'(w_i)} = \sum_{j=1}^{m} \frac{p_j(a_i)}{u'(w_{ij})}$$

---

19. Note, in passing, that this equality proves the memory effect. Consider indeed i and k such that for all j, $w_{ij} = w_{kj}$; then it must be that $a_i = a_k$, so

$$\frac{1}{u'(w_i)} = \sum_{j=1}^{m} \frac{p_j(a_i)}{u'(w_{ij})} = \sum_{j=1}^{m} \frac{p_j(a_k)}{u'(w_{kj})} = \frac{1}{u'(w_k)}$$

which implies that $w_i = w_k$. The second-period wages can therefore only be independent of the first-period outcome if the first-period wages are constant, which would imply that the Principal has given up trying to get the Agent to put in some effort.

By Jensen's inequality[20] applied to the convex function $x \to 1/x$,

$$\sum_{j=1}^{m} \frac{p_j(a_i)}{u'(w_{ij})} \geq \frac{1}{\sum_{j=1}^{m} p_j(a_i)u'(w_{ij})}$$

Therefore

$$u'(w_i) \leq \sum_{j=1}^{m} p_j(a_i)u'(w_{ij})$$

which implies as announced that the Agent would want to save if he could.[21]

This result makes it somewhat difficult to interpret the model as a situation in which the Agent has no access to credit markets. Indeed, while it is clear that many economic agents cannot borrow as they would like, it is not easy to see what could prevent them from saving to their heart's content. This leads us to examine the case in which the Principal in fact dictates his savings to the Agent so that both wages and consumptions are determined by the contract. This in fact links different periods exactly as short-term commitment does when the Agent cannot save or borrow. Thus we should expect that the no commitment optimum coincides with the full commitment optimum. Malcolmson-Spinnewyn (1988) show that such is indeed the case.

---

20. Recall that Jensen's inequality states that if X is a random variable and f is a convex function, then

$Ef(X) \geq f(EX)$.

21. Let $F(s)$ be the utility the Agent gets by saving s at the market interest rate $r = 1/\delta - 1$; then

$$F(s) = u(w_i - s) + \delta \sum_{j=1}^{m} p_j(a_i)u\left(w_{ij} + \frac{s}{\delta}\right)$$

and the inequality on marginal utilities in the text is simply $F'(0) \geq 0$.

Unfortunately, not many real-world situations seem to fit this model. The first one is sharecropping in developing countries. Sharecropping is an agreement between a landlord and his tenant according to which the landlord lets the tenant cultivate his land and they share the proceeds from the crop. While it has almost disappeared from developed countries, it is still very common in the Third World. Since credit markets are underdeveloped in these countries, the tenant usually can only get credit from his landlord, which justifies using the model above. Another candidate is the case when the Agent is a firm and the Principal is one of its main shareholders or bankers; however, this interaction has many special features that do not make it a very convincing example.

Free Access to Credit

Let us now turn to the polar case in which the Agent can save and borrow as he wishes. I will assume that the Principal cannot observe the Agent's savings. Let s_{T-1} denote the savings of the Agent in period $(T - 1)$ (which depend of course on the whole past history) and $r = 1/\delta - 1$ the market interest rate. Then the utility function of the Agent in period T, expressed as a function of the wage he gets from the Principal, is

$$U(w_T; s_{T-1}) = u(w_T + (1 + r)s_{T-1})$$

which depends on his past savings s_{T-1}.

Since the Principal does not observe s_{T-1}, he faces at the beginning of period T an Agent whose utility function he does not know:[22] An adverse selection problem emerges on top of the moral hazard problem.[23] This has several important consequences. The first one is that as in all adverse selection models, full commitment

22. The only exception is when the Agent's utility function is CARA, which excludes wealth effects and therefore the emergence of adverse selection. This case is dealt with by Fudenberg-Holmstrom-Milgrom (1990).
23. Note that uncertainty as to the Agent's characteristics is created endogenously by his past actions, whereas it is exogenous in the standard adverse selection model.

and long-term commitment lead to different solutions: The full commitment optimum is not renegotiation proof. As argued in section 6.4, we should therefore concentrate on the long-term optimum.

Unfortunately, there are very few results so far on the long-term optimum with free savings. Chiappori-Macho-Rey-Salanié (1994) show the following striking result: If the long-term optimum only involves pure strategies, then it can only implement the cost-minimizing action from the second period onward. To see this, assume that $T = 2$ and use the same notation as above, with in addition s_j as the savings when the first-period outcome is j and a_0 the optimal action in the first period. Now assume that the optimal contract implements a_i in the second period after the first-period outcome was i. If a_i is not the cost-minimizing action, then at least one second-period incentive constraint must be binding: There exists an a' such that

$$\sum_j p_j(a_i)u\left(w_{ij} + \frac{s_i}{\delta}\right) - a_i = \sum_j p_j(a')u\left(w_{ij} + \frac{s_i}{\delta}\right) - a'$$

Let s' be the optimal savings when the Agent chooses a', namely s' maximizes over s,

$$u(w_i - s) + \delta\left(\sum_j p_j(a')u\left(w_{ij} + \frac{s}{\delta}\right) - a'\right)$$

Now assume that instead of responding to the optimal contract (w_i, w_{ij}) with (a_0, s_i, a_i), the Agent responds with (a_0', s_i', a_i') which coincides with (a_0, s_i, a_i) except that $a_i' = a'$ and $s_i' = s'$. We will show that this improves the Agent's expected utility. Indeed we have

$$\sum_j p_j(a_0)\left(u(w_j - s_j) - a_0 + \delta\left(\sum_k p_k(a_j)u\left(w_{jk} + \frac{s_j}{\delta}\right) - a_j\right)\right)$$

$$= \sum_j p_j(a_0')\left(u(w_j - s_j) - a_0' + \delta\left(\sum_k p_k(a_j')u\left(w_{jk} + \frac{s_j}{\delta}\right) - a_j'\right)\right)$$

$$< \sum_j p_j(a_0')\left(u(w_j - s_j') - a_0' + \delta\left(\sum_k p_k(a_j')u\left(w_{jk} + \frac{s_j'}{\delta}\right) - a_j'\right)\right),$$

where the first equality follows from the definition of a' and the inequality holds (generically) because s' is a better choice of savings than s given a'.

Since this inequality violates the first-period incentive constraint, our premise that a_i was not the cost-minimizing action must be wrong. The conclusion follows immediately.[24]

This is an unwelcome result. Pure strategies have two advantages: They are much simpler to compute and thus more "reasonable," and the long-term optimum in pure strategies is implementable through spot contracts, as can also be shown in this model.[25] However, since the long-term optimum in pure strategies gives such low-powered incentives to the Agent, it must be that the optimum involves mixed strategies. Unfortunately, no analogue of the Spence-Mirrlees condition can be expected to hold in that model, so characterizing the optimum is quite beyond us.

Conclusion

This rapid survey of finitely repeated moral hazard models shows that there is still much work to be done in this area. Both polar assumptions of no access to credit or free access to credit lead us to distressing conclusions. In the first case, the Agent is prevented from saving at the optimum. In the second case, the optimum must involve mixed strategies if it is to have good incentive properties.

There are nevertheless two general conclusions to be drawn, and both result from the importance of consumption smoothing. The first one concerns the memory effect: Consumption in any given period will depend on the whole history of past outcomes. Second, the relative efficiency of different degrees of commitment is determined by their ability to smooth the Agent's consumption.

---

24. Note that this result is not unlike that by Fudenberg-Tirole (1990) presented in section 6.5.1, in which effort cannot be implemented with probability one. In both cases the renegotiation constraints are to blame.

25. The latter result is not very surprising, since the Agent can smooth his consumption optimally through the credit markets.

References

Aghion, P., and P. Bolton. 1987. Contracts as a barrier to entry. *American Economic Review* 77:388–401.

Baron, D., and D. Besanko . 1984. Regulation and information in a continuing relationship. *Information Economics and Policy* 1:267–302.

Brander, J., and B. Spencer. 1985. Export subsidies and international market share rivalry. *Journal of International Economics* 18:83–100.

Caillaud, B., B. Jullien, and P. Picard. 1995. Competing vertical structures: Precommitment and renegotiation. *Econometrica* 63:621–46.

Chiappori, P.-A., I. Macho, P. Rey, and B. Salanié. 1994. Repeated moral hazard: The role of memory, commitment, and the access to credit markets. *European Economic Review* 38:1527–53.

Dewatripont, M. 1988. Commitment through renegotiation-proof contracts with third parties. *Review of Economic Studies* 55:377–90.

Dewatripont, M. 1989. Renegotiation and information revelation over time: The case of optimal labor contracts. *Quarterly Journal of Economics* 104:589–619.

Fershtman, C., and K. Judd. 1987. Equilibrium incentives in oligopoly. *American Economic Review* 77:927–40.

Freixas, X., R. Guesnerie, and J. Tirole. 1985. Planning under incomplete information and the ratchet effect. *Review of Economic Studies* 52:173–92.

Fudenberg, D., B. Holmstrom, and P. Milgrom. 1990. Short-term contracts and long-term agency relationships. *Journal of Economic Theory* 51:1–31.

Fudenberg, D., and J. Tirole. 1990. Moral hazard and renegotiation in agency contracts. *Econometrica* 58:1279–1320.

Hart, O., and J. Tirole. 1988. Contract renegotiation and coasian dynamics. *Review of Economic Studies* 55:509–40.

Katz, M. 1986. Game-playing agents: Unobservable contracts as precommitment. *Rand Journal of Economics* 22:307–28.

Laffont, J.-J., and J. Tirole. 1987. Comparative statics of the optimal dynamic incentives contract. *European Economic Review* 31:901–26.

Laffont, J.-J., and J. Tirole. 1990. Adverse selection and renegotiation in procurement. *Review of Economic Studies* 75:597–626.

Laffont, J.-J., and J. Tirole. 1993. *A Theory of Incentives in Procurement and Regulation.* Cambridge: MIT Press.

Malcolmson, J., and F. Spinnewyn. 1988. The multiperiod Principal-Agent problem. *Review of Economic Studies* 55:391–408.

Rey, P., and B. Salanié. 1990. Long-term, short-term and renegotiation: On the value of commitment in contracting. *Econometrica* 58:597–619.

Rey, P., and B. Salanié. 1996. On the value of commitment in contracting with asymmetric information. *Econometrica* 64:1395–1414.

Rogerson, W. 1985. Repeated moral hazard. *Econometrica* 53:69–76.

Rubinstein, A., and M. Yaari. 1983. Insurance and moral hazard. *Journal of Economic Theory* 14:441–52.

Schelling, T. 1960. *The Strategy of Conflict.* Cambridge: Harvard University Press.

7   Incomplete Contracts

I have assumed so far that contracts are complete. This is obviously a very strong assumption, since it implies that all contingencies that may affect the contractual relationship are taken into account in the contract. In the real world, negotiating a contract is a costly business, which mobilizes managers and lawyers. It must therefore be that at some point, the cost of taking into account an improbable contingency outweighs the benefits of writing a specific clause in the contract; the contract should then be signed without this clause. The unability (or unwillingness) of courts or other third parties to verify ex post the values taken by certain variables observed by all contractants is another reason why contracts will be incomplete: It is no use conditioning the contract on a variable if nobody can settle the disputes that may arise. Even if we abstract from the costs associated with negotiating and writing the contract and from the constraints due to the legal system, bounded rationality may force the parties to neglect some variables whose effect on the relationship they find difficult to evaluate. Finally, it is sometimes difficult or even impossible to assign a probability to some relevant events and thus to condition the clauses of the contract on these events, but that would lead us into bounded rationality considerations that would not be very productive at this stage, given that the profession has made very little progress in modeling them.

For all of these reasons, contracts typically only take into account a limited number of variables that may be the most relevant ones, or simply those that are most easily verifiable by a court. During the relationship, some unforeseen contingencies[1] may therefore arise; insofar as these contingencies have an impact on the conditions of the relationship and the contract gives no clue as to how the parties should react, they will want to renegotiate the contract.

Renegotiation therefore has a very different meaning when contracts are complete and when they are incomplete. We saw in chapter 6 that when contracts are complete, the ability to renegotiate acts as an ex ante constraint on the Principal's program, and it will therefore often bring an efficiency loss. Moreover the renegotiation-proofness principle shows that long-term contracts need never be renegotiated in equilibrium. On the other hand, renegotiation allows the parties to react to unforeseen contingencies when contracts are incomplete; renegotiation may therefore be socially useful, and it will actually take place in equilibrium.

The theory of incomplete contracts in many ways builds on and formalizes the intuitions of transaction cost economics, as created by Coase and Williamson.[2] Transaction cost economics accepts that agents are opportunistic but claims that they are boundedly rational, so contracts will be incomplete. It also insists that many assets are relationship-specific in that they have little value outside the relationship under study. Since many investments (especially investments in human capital) in relationship-specific assets are non-verifiable, parties will fear that they may be expropriated of the surplus created by these specific investments and thus they will tend to underinvest; this is the famous *hold up* problem, to which we will return in section 7.2.

---

1. I just mean here, with a slight abuse of vocabulary, contingencies that the contract does not condition upon.

2. Beginning with the 1937 paper by Coase on *The Nature of the Firm* (this and other famous papers by Coase are reprinted in Coase 1988). Williamson (1989) gives a useful survey of transaction cost economics.

The study of incomplete contracts is still at a preliminary stage; the models used by different authors are rarely comparable, and the general foundations of the theory have not been established yet. As in most of the literature, I will concentrate here on examining some very simple cases where information is symmetric: All variables are observed by all parties, but some of them may not be included in a contract. We will say that such variables are observable but nonverifiable, meaning that no court or other third party will accept to arbitrate a claim based on the value taken by these variables. The symmetric information assumption distinguishes this chapter from all the rest of this book;[3] still it will allow us to isolate the phenomena that are due to contract incompleteness. It also greatly simplifies the analysis of renegotiation: As shown in section 6.4, this is quite complex when information is asymmetric.

7.1   Observable but Nonverifiable Effort

Let us come back to the one-period moral hazard model studied in chapter 5, but we assume now that action a is observable but non-verifiable. As in the traditional moral hazard model, it can therefore not be specified in a contract.

With full commitment the optimal contract is defined by the equations we studied in chapter 5. Assume, to the contrary, that parties may renegotiate after the Principal observes the action chosen by the Agent. As in the Fudenberg-Tirole model studied in section 6.5.1, the Principal must now offer a certain (constant) wage to the Agent so as to insure him completely.[4]

Let a_i be an action that is implementable in the classical model so that there exists a wage schedule w^* such that

---

3. At a theoretical level, it may, however, be noted that the nonverifiability assumption often implicitly refers to asymmetric information between the parties and the third party: The latter cannot check the value of a variable because it cannot observe it.

4. I again assume here that the Principal is risk-neutral and the Agent is risk-averse.

$$\sum_{j=1}^{m} p_{ij}u(w_j^*) - a_i = \max_{k} \left(\sum_{j=1}^{m} p_{kj}u(w_j^*) - a_k \right) \geq \underline{U}$$

When the action is observable but nonverifiable, the Principal can propose the contract w^* to the Agent, observe his chosen action a_k, and then propose him a wage $\overline{w}_k$ independent of the outcome x such that

$$u(\overline{w}_k) = \sum_{j=1}^{m} p_{kj}u(w_j^*)$$

The Agent accepts the renegotiation (he is indeed indifferent between the old contract and the new one); ex ante, the new contract gives him exactly the same incentives as the first one: The Agent must compute the value of k that maximizes

$$u(\overline{w}_k) - a_k$$

which, by construction, equals

$$\sum_{j=1}^{m} p_{kj}u(w_j^*) - a_k$$

and thus the Agent will choose action a_i.

But since u is concave, Jensen's inequality shows that for all k

$$\sum_{j=1}^{m} p_{kj}u(w_j^*) \leq u\left(\sum_{j=1}^{m} p_{kj}w_j^* \right)$$

and thus

$$\overline{w}_k = u^{-1}\left(\sum_{j=1}^{m} p_{kj}u(w_j^*) \right) \leq \sum_{j=1}^{m} p_{kj}w_j^*$$

Implementing the optimal action a_i therefore is less costly than in the classical model: Renegotiation allows the Principal to insure the

Agent perfectly and thus makes it easier for him to choose an incentive wage schedule. This result is not terribly surprising, since the action here is observable, contrary to the classical model. However, we could prove a stronger result: Under some conditions the Principal can even implement the first-best optimum (see Hermalin-Katz 1991).

This very simple model illustrates well the contrast between complete contracts and incomplete contracts: Whereas the ability to renegotiate must be analyzed as a constraint when contracts are complete, it increases the efficiency of the contractual relationship when they are incomplete. This is a very general conclusion.[5]

7.2 Property and Residual Control Rights

In a world of complete contracts, the allocation of property rights only matters for distributive purposes: It has no bearing on efficiency. Complete contracts indeed can specify in full detail what each party must do in each state of the world and how the surplus should be shared. Thus, if a firm M (the manufacturer) produces computers that a firm D (the dealer) sells to the public, it is socially indifferent whether the two firms are legally distinct, whether M buys D or whether D buys M. Indeed, the theory of complete contracts appears to have nothing to say on what pins down the boundaries of firms.

This description of the economic world hardly seems realistic: The boundaries of firms are obviously not random. When business leaders or judges discuss vertical integration, they constantly refer to

---

5. Some economists would deny that the Hermalin-Katz paper belongs to the incomplete contracts literature. They argue that when effort is observable but not verifiable, revelation games can be designed that effectively bypass its nonverifiability. Thus Hermalin-Katz just found a simple way to implement the optimum by using renegotiation. As section 7.4 will show, I am sympathetic to that view. I still included the Hermalin-Katz model in this chapter because I think it is a good example of circumstances in which the ability to renegotiate may become an asset.

efficiency concepts. The theory of incomplete contracts will allow us to give this question a central role and to link them to the legal tradition. Roman law defined property rights as the combination of *usus* (the right to use the good), *fructus* (the right to what it produces), and *abusus* (the right to sell or give away the good). Closer to us, the anglo-saxon legal tradition defines property rights as *residual control rights*: When an unforeseen contingency occurs, the owner has the right to decide how the good should be used (see Grossman-Hart 1986). The owner also gets exclusive rights on all income streams that have not been shared in advance by a contract. These rights clearly have no value if contracts are complete, since no unforeseen contingency then ever arises. They only matter if contracts are incomplete.[6]

Assume, for instance, that one at least of the parties can make a *specific investment*, that is, an investment that

- increases the productivity of the relationship under study,
- has a lower value outside of this relationship,
- is costly for the party that makes it.

We will assume that specific investments are observable by all parties but are nonverifiable. Whatever the allocation of property rights, the cost of the investment is born by the party who makes it.[7] On the other hand, how the resulting income stream is shared depends on property rights. Only the owner receives the full benefit of his investment, while other parties, who do not receive all of the surplus generated by their investments, will tend to underinvest. This is the celebrated *hold up* problem.

The notions of specific investments and hold ups are often illustrated by the relationship between Fisher Bodies, an American maker

---

6. I do not claim to be an expert on legal matters, much less on anglo-saxon law. I urge the reader to refer to the interesting paper by Schwartz (1992).
7. Think, for instance, of investments in human capital.

of car parts, and General Motors.[8] In the 1920s Fisher Bodies was producing car doors for General Motors; it therefore invested in some rather specialized machine tools and organized its production so as to respond best to the needs of General Motors. Clearly Fisher Bodies would have lost a considerable part of the value of its investments if it had left General Motors for another car maker. Therefore a contract signed in 1919 gave Fisher Bodies a ten-year exclusive dealing clause to protect it from being held up by General Motors. On the other hand, this gave Fisher Bodies the possibility of raising prices outrageously; to prevent this, the contract also contained a cost-plus clause. It turned out, however, that Fisher Bodies manipulated the price-protection clause by choosing a very low capital intensity and locating its plants far from those of General Motors. General Motors thus was effectively held up by Fisher Bodies and eventually bought it in 1926.

Let us illustrate these concepts with an example drawn from Holmstrom-Tirole (1989). Assume that the computer manufacturer M and his dealer D have agreed on a contract, which we will use as a benchmark. M then decides to invest in research and development of an innovation that will increase the market value of his computers. The increase in value expected from this innovation is a random variable v. The dealer, however, does not have to accept this innovation; it will indeed force him to modify his product line and his commercial practices, which entails a random cost c. The variable v may take two values: 2 and 4. M can influence the probability distribution of v by making a specific investment x that costs him x^2 but ensures that the probability that $v = 4$ is x. Similarly c may be 1 or 3, and D can ensure that the probability of $c = 1$ is y by making a specific investment y that costs him y^2.

We will assume that the four variables x, y, v, and c, once realized, are observed by both parties but are nonverifiable. No contract will

---

8. This story is told at length in the classic paper by Klein-Crawford-Alchian (1978).

therefore be signed ex ante. On the other hand, the two parties may renegotiate[9] after observing v and c. For a given allocation of property rights, the game is as follows:

- M and D choose the values of x and y and pay the corresponding costs.
- M and D observe the values taken by v and c.
- M and D renegotiate to decide whether or not the innovative computer is to be put on sale and, if yes, how to share the surplus.

First note that the innovation will be sold in the three cases (out of four) where v is larger than c; the exception is the case where $v = 2$ and $c = 3$, which has probability $(1 - x)(1 - y)$. We will denote by $S(x, y)$ the expected gross social surplus, that is,

$$\begin{aligned} S(x, y) &= E\left(\max (v - c, 0) \mid x, y\right) \\ &= 3xy + x(1 - y) + (1 - x)y \\ &= xy + x + y \end{aligned}$$

First consider the *social optimum*, which is obtained by maximizing the net expected social surplus, or

$$\max_{x, y} \left(S(x,y) - x^2 - y^2\right)$$

which gives $x = y = 1$ and a net expected social surplus $W = 1$. The social optimum therefore here consists of making the maximal investments so as to ensure that the most favorable case ($v = 4, c = 1$) obtains and thus that the innovation is sold with probability one.

Now consider the *nonintegrated* case in which M and D are distinct legal entities. We will assume that when renegotiating, M and D decide to share the gross expected social surplus equally (e.g., the Nash bargaining solution). Then M chooses his investment x by maximizing

---

9. Strictly speaking, there is nothing to renegotiate here.

$$\frac{S(x, y)}{2} - x^2$$

and y maximizes

$$\frac{S(x, y)}{2} - y^2$$

The Nash equilibrium of this game gives $x = y = 1/3$ and $W = 5/9$. Both parties therefore underinvest, since they know that they can only get half of the income stream generated by their investments.

Now assume that M buys D (*downstream integration*). D then does not invest at all, since he would incur the investment costs and have no right on the surplus his investment generates. Therefore $y = 0$ and $c = 3$. M chooses the level x of his investment by maximizing

$$S(x, 0) - x^2$$

whence $x = 1/2$ and $W = 1/4$. Compared to the nonintegrated case, D underinvests and M overinvests.

The computations are very similar when D buys M (*upstream integration*); we then get $x = 0$, $y = 1/2$, and $W = 1/2$. This time M underinvests and D overinvests.

In this example the social surplus is therefore smaller if firms are integrated: The costs of integration outweigh its benefits. This conclusion clearly is very sensitive to the value of the parameters and the exact specification of the model: firms do sometimes integrate![10] The aim of this model is only to show that when contracts are incomplete, some allocations of property rights may be more efficient than others.

---

10. As in the case of Fisher Bodies, which was eventually bought by General Motors. Hart (1995, ch. 2) studies a similar but more general model and derives conditions for either of the three allocations of property rights (nonintegration, downstream integration, and upstream integration) to be optimal.

7.3   Contract Incompleteness and Underinvestment

In the example we just studied, the incompleteness of contracts always leads to underinvestment by both parties (compared to the social optimum), whatever the allocation of property rights. This theme is already present in Grout (1984); Hart-Moore (1988) find a similar result in a more general and more abstract model. The idea that when contracts are incomplete, the parties will tend to underinvest in specific assets is the basis for Williamson's intuitions. However, Aghion-Dewatripont-Rey (1994) (hereafter ADR) show that this conclusion strongly depends on how the contractual *statu quo* is defined and on the allocation of bargaining power at the renegotiating stage.

• The contractual *statu quo* is the agreement that parties fall back on if they cannot agree during renegotiation. In our example this "default" contract was given a priori; ADR assume, to the contrary, that it can be chosen arbitrarily.

• We assumed in our example that the surplus generated by the renegotiation were shared equally between both parties. ADR use the standard assumption of Principal-Agent models: One of the parties has all the bargaining power when renegotiating and will therefore appropriate the whole surplus.

ADR show that under these assumptions, there exist simple contracts that implement the socially optimal levels of specific investment.

Consider, for instance, a buyer B and a seller S who exchange q units of a good at a price p. The buyer can make a specific investment i that increases the surplus he obtains by consuming the good; similarly the seller may reduce his production costs by making a specific investment j. As in the model of the preceding section, we will assume that the specific investments are affected by noises ε and η. The utility functions are

$$U_B = s(q, i, \varepsilon) - p - \psi(i)$$

for the buyer and

$$U_S = p - c(q, j, \eta) - \varphi(j)$$

for the seller, where s is increasing and concave in (q, i), c is increasing in q, decreasing in j and convex in (q, j), and ψ and φ are increasing and convex.

At the beginning of the game, the parties sign a contract, they then make investments i and j, and later the noises ε and η are realized. We will assume that all variables are observable but that only the variables p and q are verifiable and therefore can figure in a contract.

The efficient ex post trade is given by maximizing $(U_B + U_S)$. It is therefore the quantity $q^*(i, j, \varepsilon, \eta)$ such that

$$\frac{\partial s}{\partial q}(q^*(i, j, \varepsilon, \eta), i, \varepsilon) = \frac{\partial c}{\partial q}(q^*(i, j, \varepsilon, \eta), j, \eta)$$

It is of course impossible to reach this level of trade with the initial contract, since that can only specify an unconditional price-quantity pair (p_0, q_0). On the other hand, bilateral renegotiation will allow us to implement $q^*(i, j, \varepsilon, \eta)$ after i and j have been chosen and the noises have realized.[11]

Assume, to fix ideas, that the whole surplus of the renegotiation goes to the seller. Since renegotiation is assumed to be efficient, it will lead to the quantity $q^*(i, j, \varepsilon, \eta)$ and to the price p such that

$$p - c(q^*(i, j, \varepsilon, \eta), j, \eta) = p_0 - c(q_0, j, \eta) + G$$

where G is the gain from renegotiation, or

$$G = (s(q^*(i, j, \varepsilon, \eta), i, \varepsilon) - c(q^*(i, j, \varepsilon, \eta), j, \eta)) - (s(q_0, i, \varepsilon) - c(q_0, j, \eta))$$

After the renegotiation the buyer therefore gets utility

$$U_B = s(q_0, i, \varepsilon) - p_0 - \psi(i)$$

---

11. Information then is perfect, so we may safely assume that renegotiation leads to the efficient quantity.

while the seller achieves utility

$$U_S = p_0 + s(q^*(i, j, \varepsilon, \eta), i, \varepsilon) - s(q_0, i, \varepsilon) - c(q^*(i, j, \varepsilon, \eta), j, \eta) - \varphi(j)$$

Now let i^* and j^* be the optimal investment levels, which maximize

$$E_{\varepsilon,\eta}\Big(s(q^*(i, j, \varepsilon, \eta), i, \varepsilon) - c(q^*(i, j, \varepsilon, \eta), j, \eta) - \psi(i) - \varphi(j)\Big)$$

and let the quantity q_0 be given by

$$E_\varepsilon \frac{\partial s}{\partial i}(q_0, i^*, \varepsilon) = \psi'(i^*)$$

We will now prove that if the initial contract prescribes the quantity q_0, then the agents will choose the optimal investment levels i^* and j^*. First note that after the renegotiation the buyer's utility U_B does not depend on j; the seller therefore gets all the surplus from his own investment j, which automatically makes him choose the optimal level j^*. As for the buyer, maximizing the expected utility he gets after the renegotiation makes him choose an i such that

$$E_\varepsilon \frac{\partial s}{\partial i}(q_0, i, \varepsilon) = \psi'(i)$$

and by our definition of q_0, we get $i = i^*$.

This result can be understood by noting that we have here two instruments (bargaining power and the initial contract) to reach the two investment targets.[12] On the other hand, Hart-Moore (1988) fix the initial contract, and Grout (1984) adopts Nash bargaining; these authors therefore only have one instrument available, which explains why they obtain underinvestment results.

There therefore is no underinvestment if the initial contract is well chosen and all bargaining power is given to one of the parties when renegotiating. The reader can thus check that in the model of section 7.2 the investments made in the nonintegrated case are efficient if

12. Nöldeke-Schmidt (1995) rely on similar assumptions to derive an efficient investment result in the Hart-Moore (1988) model.

the initial contract prescribes that the innovation will be made[13] and if all surplus from the renegotiation is given to either one of the two parties.

7.4   Concluding Remarks

The ADR paper has not closed the debate on underinvestment versus efficient investment. Proponents of the underinvestment results argue that in many cases the characteristics of the good to be traded are so numerous that it will effectively be impossible to describe it ex ante and therefore to write an initial contract (q_0, p_0) with a nonzero q_0. Then the underinvestment result will prevail again. Still this shows that the results obtained so far in the theory of incomplete contracts are very sensitive to the fine details of modeling. This is all the more worrying as the foundations of incomplete contracting are not well-established yet. Tirole (1994) argues that there is a tension between two conflicting views of rationality in that literature. On the one hand, unmodeled bounded rationality considerations are usually invoked to explain why complete contracts cannot be written and why some contingencies cannot be taken into account. On the other hand, all papers in this field make use of the principle of dynamic programming, which presumes a strong dose of rationality. Building on results in Maskin-Tirole (1996), Tirole shows that if renegotiation can be prevented, using sophisticated message games will allow the parties to achieve the same payoffs as when contracts are complete. The reason is that so long as all variables are observed by both parties (a maintained hypothesis of the literature so far), their nonverifiability can be circumvented by playing revelation games adapted from the literature on subgame-perfect implementation. In particular, the hold-up problem can be solved in that context so that underinvestment need never arise.

---

13. Whereas in section 7.2 we implicitly assumed that the initial contract does not arrange for the innovation to be made.

This result challenges the common view about incomplete contracting. It suggests three avenues for research. The first one consists in building an explicit theory of bounded rationality and studying its implications for contracting. Unfortunately, while many authors have insisted on the need for such an approach, little progress has been made yet. Another way to bypass the Maskin-Tirole result is to make the usual assumption that multilateral renegotiation cannot be prevented; the intuition here is that as the contracting environment becomes more complex, renegotiation will constrain the exchange of messages so much that the outcome of standard incomplete contracts will be achieved in the limit (see Segal 1997 for a good example). The third approach consists in challenging the received wisdom which claims that complete contracts cannot explain phenomena such as authority and property rights; Tirole indeed exhibits a model in which, with renegotiation allowed, the optimal complete contract can be implemented by an allocation of property rights typical of simple incomplete contracts.

Finally, there is also a case to be made for a more practical-minded attack on incomplete contracting that completely disregards the debate on their foundations and goes on to explore their consequences on models of the firm. The recent book by Hart (1995) shows that many interesting insights can be obtained in this way. In my view, proponents of this approach should eventually study the consequences of incomplete contracting when information is asymmetric. Recall that in that case renegotiation need not be efficient a priori, which raises a host of new problems.

References

Aghion, P., M. Dewatripont, and P. Rey. 1994. Renegotiation design with unverifiable information. *Econometrica* 62:257–82.

Coase, R. 1988. *The Firm, the Market, and the Law.* Chicago: University of Chicago Press.

Grossman, S., and O. Hart. 1986. The costs and benefits of ownership: A theory of vertical and lateral integration. *Journal of Political Economy* 94:691–719.

Grout, P. 1984. Investment and wages in the absence of binding contracts: A Nash bargaining approach. *Econometrica* 52:449–60.

Hart, O. 1995. *Firms, Contracts, and Financial Structure*, Oxford: Oxford University Press.

Hart, O., and J. Moore. 1988. Incomplete contracts and renegotiation. *Econometrica* 56:755–85.

Hermalin, B., and M. Katz. 1991. Moral hazard and verifiability: The effects of renegotiation in agency. *Econometrica* 59:1735–53.

Holmstrom, B., and J. Tirole. 1989. The theory of the firm. *Handbook of Industrial Organization*, vol. 1. Amsterdam: North-Holland.

Klein, B., R. Crawford, and A. Alchian. 1978. Vertical integration, appropriable rents and the competitive contracting process. *Journal of Law and Economics* 21:297–326.

Maskin, E., and J. Tirole. 1996. Unforeseen contingencies, property rights, and incomplete contracts. Mimeo. IDEI.

Nöldeke, G., and K. Schmidt. 1995. Option contracts and renegotiation: A solution to the hold-up problem. *Rand Journal of Economics* 26:163–79.

Schwartz, A. 1992. Legal contract theories and incomplete contracts. In *Contract Economics*, L. Werin and H. Wijkander, eds. Oxford: Basil Blackwell.

Segal, I. 1997. Complexity and renegotiation: A foundation for incomplete contracts. Forthcoming in the *Review of Economic Studies*.

Tirole, J. 1994. Incomplete contracts: Where do we stand? Mimeo. IDEI.

Williamson, O. 1989. Transaction cost economics. *Handbook of Industrial Organization*, vol. 1. Amsterdam: North-Holland.

8 Some Empirical Work

It is a capital mistake to theorise before one has data.
Arthur Conan Doyle, *A Scandal in Bohemia.*

I hope to have convinced the reader by now that the explosive development of the theory of contracts since the early 1970s has produced many increasingly more realistic models that shed light on many fields of economic activity. However, it is only fair to say that the increasing sophistication of the theory has not gone hand in hand with the empirical validation of the models. Many papers consist of theoretical analyses with little attention to the facts.[1] Others state so-called stylized facts often based on anecdotal evidence and go on to study a model from which these stylized facts can be derived. A rather small number of authors derive qualitative predictions from the theory and go on to test them on actual data. But contrary to most other fields of economic theory, econometrics has been very rarely used to check the predictions of the theory of contracts. A growing number of scholars have come to deplore this state of affairs. After all, even if the philosophy of science held by Sherlock Holmes is somewhat outdated, it does seem that we should do more to exploit whatever data we can lay our hands on.

This chapter will present what I think is promising work in the econometrics of contracts. Most of this work is very recent, so my

---

1. Obviously the division of labor requires that there should be such papers.

presentation of it will reflect my own views of what is important. In particular, I will only briefly mention reduced-form econometric work. In such work a qualitative prediction is derived and tested in an econometric model that does not directly conform with the economic model that underlies the prediction. Reduced-form econometrics is easy to implement, since it usually neglects, for instance, the nonlinearities of most economic models. However, it does not allow the econometrician to estimate the deep parameters of the model. For this reason I think structural econometrics, which directly estimates the equations of the economic model, is more appealing.[2] Of course it is also much more costly, though, recent advances in nonlinear econometrics and in computer power make it feasible to estimate structural models that would have been out of reach a few years ago.

In the first section of this chapter, I will show how the standard adverse selection model of chapter 2 can be estimated; I also discuss the burgeoning recent work on auctions. The second section discusses the estimation of moral hazard models, where even less work has been done; it shows that exploiting the dynamic properties of these models and using insurance data are two promising avenues for research.

I have tried to keep the presentation here as simple as possible, but the reader should be warned that this chapter presupposes a little familiarity with standard econometric concepts and methods.

8.1 Adverse Selection Models

8.1.1 The Standard Model

Let us return to the model studied in section 2.3.2 and assume that the Principal's cost function depends on wage w and a parameter

---

2. This is not to deny that much interesting work has been done in reduced-form econometrics on contracts. I will give a few pointers to this burgeoning literature in this chapter.

vector β, while the Agent's utility function depends on a parameter vector a. Thus their objective functions are

$$t - C(q, w, \beta)$$

for the Principal and

$$u(q, \theta, a) - t$$

for the Agent, where q is a quality or quantity index and t is a monetary transfer. The wage w is observed by both parties and by the econometrician,[3] while a and β are observed by both parties but not by the econometrician, who wants to estimate them from the data. The observational status of θ depends on our assumptions. First consider model S (for symmetric information) in which both Principal and Agent observe θ. Then we obtain by maximizing the total surplus

$$\frac{\partial u}{\partial q}(q^S, \theta, a) = \frac{\partial C}{\partial q}(q^S, w, \beta) + \sigma\varepsilon$$

where an error term has been appended to the relationship to take into account specification errors, imperfect data observation, and all the other reasons that imply that the relationship will not hold exactly in the data. This implicitly defines the solution $q^S(\theta, w, a, \beta, \sigma, \varepsilon)$ and allows us to compute the likelihood function $l^S(q, w, a, \beta, \sigma; \theta)$, which is conditional on θ.

Now consider the more interesting model A (for asymmetric information) in which only the Agent knows θ and the Principal has a prior given by a probability distribution function f and a cumulative distribution function F on $[\underline{\theta}, \overline{\theta}]$. In that case we know from chapter 2 that under the appropriate hazard rate condition, the solution is given by

$$\frac{\partial u}{\partial q}(q^A, \theta, a) = \frac{\partial C}{\partial q}(q^A, w, \beta) + \frac{\partial^2 u}{\partial q \partial \theta}(q^A, \theta, a)\frac{1 - F(\theta)}{f(\theta)} + \sigma\varepsilon$$

---

3. In econometric terms, w is an exogenous variable.

which generates $q^A(\theta, (1 - F(\theta))/f(\theta), w, a, \beta, \sigma, \varepsilon)$ and the likelihood function $l^A(q, w, a, \beta, \sigma; \theta, (1 - F(\theta))/f(\theta))$. Note that the latter is conditional both on θ and on $(1 - F(\theta))/f(\theta)$.

Assume that we have data on n relationships between Principals and Agents that are identical except for the wage rate[4] w so that our sample is $(q_i, w_i)_{i=1}^{n}$. The difficulty here is that we do not know θ or f, even in model S in which both parties observe θ. In econometric terms θ is an unobserved heterogeneity parameter, and we must integrate over it. To do this, we must find a functional form for f that is flexible enough, given that we have very little idea of what the Principal's prior may look like. One solution is to choose a kernel that is an even function with compact support and that integrates to one,[5] to choose a small integer J, and to approximate f with

$$f_J(\theta) = \sum_{j=1}^{J} \frac{k_j}{h_j} K\left(\frac{\theta - \tau_j}{h_j}\right)$$

where the k_j are nonnegative and sum to one and the h_j are positive. Such a f_J is a mixture of distributions shaped like the kernel K, centered around the location parameters τ_j with dispersion parameters (called *windows*) h_j, and weighted by the k_j. The parameters $(k_j, h_j, \tau_j)_{j=1}^{J}$ are to be estimated along with a, β, and σ.

We can now estimate all parameters of model S by maximizing the log-likelihood

$$\sum_{i=1}^{n} \log \int l^S(q_i, w_i, a, \beta, \sigma; \theta) f_J(\theta) d\theta$$

---

4. In real empirical work it would of course be necessary to use many more exogenous variables; however, this is irrelevant to our discussion.

5. As an example, a common choice for a kernel is the Epanechnikov kernel, which is given by

$$K(z) = \begin{cases} \dfrac{3}{4}\left(1 - z^2\right) & \text{if } |z| \leq 1 \\ 0 & \text{if } |z| > 1 \end{cases}$$

To estimate model A, we must first integrate f_J to get F_J; then we maximize

$$\sum_{i=1}^{n} \log \int l^A \left(q_i, w_i, \alpha, \beta, \sigma; \theta, \frac{1 - F_J(\theta)}{f_J(\theta)} \right) f_J(\theta) d\theta$$

These log-likelihood functions are obviously highly nonlinear and also require a numerical integration in both models; however, modern computers make it quite feasible to maximize them.

Wolak (1994) introduced this approach to study the regulation of water utilities in California in the 1980s.[6] His main conclusions are as follows:

• Nonnested tests à la Vuong (1989) favor model A over model S, indicating that asymmetric information is relevant in this regulation problem.

• Using model S instead of model A may lead the analyst to conclude wrongly that returns are increasing, whereas they are constant in model A.

• Since the capital stock of the water utilities is regulated, they tend to underinvest, which raises costs by something like 8 percent.

• The underproduction that is characteristic of adverse selection models can be evaluated to about 10 percent in the mid θ range.

Thus, Wolak's results suggest that asymmetric information may be a significant factor in some regulated industries.

8.1.2 Models of Auctions

Much empirical work has been devoted since the 1980s to the study of actual behavior of bidders in auctions. There are two strands in this literature.[7] The first one aims at testing the standard model of bidding developed in section 3.2.2 (or more elaborate extensions) by

---

6. As always, the reader should turn to Wolak's paper for all the complications that arise in a real-world implementation of the techniques presented above.

7. See Hendricks-Paarsch (1995) or Laffont (1995) for surveys of recent empirical work on auctions.

producing qualitative predictions of the theory and testing them using descriptive statistics or reduced-form econometrics; a recent example of this approach is Porter (1995). The second strand, which I will focus on here, adopts a fully structural approach to recover estimates of the parameters of the theoretical model.

The pioneering paper in this area is Laffont-Ossard-Vuong (1995).[8] I will present their approach in the context of the independent private values model with a first-price sealed-bid auction studied in section 3.2.2. Recall that there are n bidders in this model, each of which has a valuation θ_i with cumulative distribution function F on $[\underline{\theta}, \overline{\theta}]$, and these valuations are independently distributed across individuals. For estimation purposes, we will assume that F is lognormal, so that

$$\log \theta \xrightarrow{D} N(X\beta, \sigma^2)$$

where X is a vector of exogenous variables and β and σ are the parameters we want to estimate. In each auction we observe both the exogenous variables X and the value of the winning bid b_w.

We showed in section 3.2.2 that the equilibrium bidding strategies are given by

$$B(\theta_i) = \theta_i - \frac{\int_{\underline{\theta}}^{\theta_i} F(\theta)^{n-1} d\theta}{F(\theta_i)^{n-1}}$$

The winning bid is $b_w = B(\theta_{(1)})$, where $(\theta_{(1)}, \ldots, \theta_{(n)})$ is the vector of valuations arranged in decreasing order. In theory we could use this formula and the fact that we observe b_w to derive a maximum-likelihood estimator of the parameters of the distribution F. However, this is a very cumbersome way to proceed. A better idea is to rely on the expected revenue of the seller, which is

$$Eb_w = E\theta_{(2)}$$

---

8. But see also Paarsch (1992).

While it would be impossible to compute $E\theta_{(2)}$ analytically, it is easy to approximate it using simulations. To do this, draw S n-vectors $(u_1^s, \ldots, u_n^s)$ independently from the centered reduced normal distribution $N(0, 1)$. For each of these draws s, pick the second highest u_i^s and denote it $u_{(2)}^s$. Then $\exp\left(X\beta + \sigma u_{(2)}^s\right)$ is an unbiased simulator of $E\theta_{(2)}$ and a more accurate one is

$$E_S b_w(X, \beta, \sigma) = \frac{1}{S} \sum_{s=1}^{S} \exp\left(X\beta + \sigma u_{(2)}^s\right)$$

Now assume that we have data $(b_w^l, X^l)_{l=1}^{L}$ on L auctions and that these auctions can be considered to be independent.[9] A natural idea is, following Laroque-Salanié (1989), to minimize the squared distance between the observed winning bids b_w^l and the (simulated) expected theoretical bids $E_S b_w(X, \beta, \sigma)$. A simulated nonlinear least-squares estimator of β and σ thus obtains by minimizing

$$\sum_{l=1}^{L} \left(b_w^l - E_S b_w(X^l, \beta, \sigma)\right)^2$$

This gives a consistent estimator when both L and S go to infinity. In fact Laffont-Ossard-Vuong exhibit a simple bias correction that allows the estimator to be consistent and asymptotically normal when L goes to infinity even when the number of simulations S is fixed.[10] A remarkable feature of this estimation procedure is that it does not require the introduction of statistical errors; in fact the valuations θ_i play that role, since they are randomly drawn from the distribution F.

Laffont-Ossard-Vuong apply this method to auctions for eggplants in Marmande (in the southwest of France). While these auctions are descending auctions, their method still applies because it

---

9. For instance, bidders draw new private values before each auction.
10. Resorting to simulations entails an efficiency loss that is of order $1/S$ and thus can be made very small by increasing the number of simulated draws.

only relies on the formula for the seller's expected revenue, which by the revenue equivalence theorem also holds for descending auctions.[11] Their exogenous variables include, for instance, dummy variables for the size of eggplants. They obtain reasonable signs for the parameters β, and their model appears to provide a good fit to the data.

Let me make two comments on this approach. First, real-life auctions are usually much more complicated than the simple auction studied by Laffont-Ossard-Vuong. For instance, Elyakime-Laffont-Loisel-Vuong (1994) study a first-price sealed-bid auction with a secret reservation price θ_0. Then it is not possible any more to derive an analytical formula for the equilibrium bids. Let indeed G be the cumulative distribution function of θ_0 on $[\underline{\theta}, \overline{\theta}]$. Then the equilibrium bid function $B(\theta)$ satisfies the integral equation

$$B(\theta_i) = \theta_i - \frac{\int_{\underline{\theta}}^{\theta_i} F(\theta)^{n-1} G(B(\theta)) d\theta}{F(\theta_i)^{n-1} G(B(\theta_i))}$$

along with the boundary condition $B(\underline{\theta}) = \underline{\theta}$.

However, it is still possible to estimate the model nonparametrically. Let H be the cumulative distribution function of the observed bids. Then Elyakime-Laffont-Loisel-Vuong show that there exists a function ξ that only depends on G and H such that $F = H \circ \xi^{-1}$. They go on to estimate G and H nonparametrically, which gives them a nonparametric estimate of the distribution F of valuations.

Second, this line of work has so far limited its ambitions to recovering estimates of the distribution of the valuations of the bidders, without actually testing the theory against alternatives.[12] To justify this, the authors argue that the theoretical models they use make extreme assumptions (e.g., all bidders are treated symmetrically,

---

11. Another noncrucial difference in my presentation is that the seller announces a reservation price in the auctions they study.
12. For instance, it would be interesting to know whether simpler, nonstrategic theories fit the data as well.

and they never collude) and that we must develop more complete models before we can think of testing them.

8.2   Moral Hazard Models

Moral hazard models present us with a major problem. In such models the optimal incentive contract lets a measure of compensation depend on a measure of performance that is observed by both parties. Unfortunately, it is generally very difficult for the econometrician to observe performances. Take labor contracts, for instance. We know that the model predicts that the Agent's pay should depend on how well he performs, but we have very fuzzy notions of how performances are measured. Even when we know that the dependence of pay on performance is codified very strictly (as it may be in some bureaucracies), we generally cannot access such data.

There are several ways to circumvent this lack of data on performances. In some circumstances it may be clear to us how the Agent's performance must be measured. This may be the case for managerial compensation, since the goal of managers should be to maximize profits. Murphy (1986) thus takes the rate of return on common stock as a proxy of the manager's performance and uses it to test an incentive model against a learning model. Laffont-Matoussi (1995) study contracts between landlords and tenants in Tunisian agriculture. In this case the tenant's production is a natural measure of performance. They show by estimating production functions that as predicted by theory, moving from a rental contract to a sharecropping contract reduces agricultural production.

Indirect tests of the theory may also be possible. For instance, Slade (1996) applies the multitask model studied in section 5.3.7 to gasoline stations in the Vancouver area. Such stations often also act as convenience stores and/or as auto repair shops. The multitask model predicts that the shape of the optimal contract should depend on how complementary these various tasks are. This provides Slade with consequences that she goes on to test.

I will elaborate below on two other ways to estimate moral hazard models that I think should develop in the near future.

8.2.1 Using Dynamics

Even though we usually don't observe performances, we often have dynamic data on the careers of workers. Since competing theories have different consequences on the dynamics of observable variables (e.g., wages), we should be able to discriminate between them. Let me give two examples that use data on the careers of the executives of a state-owned French firm. This firm possesses all characteristics of an internal labor market: Executives are all hired at the same level, and quits and layoffs are very rare. Moreover most relative wage increases are concentrated on promotions: The only way to get a higher wage than your coworkers is to be promoted. This implies that by looking at the sequence of promotions of executives, we should get an idea of the underlying model.

Consider, for instance, the probability that an executive who has been in the firm from period 1 to period t and is currently at job level k gets promoted at the end of period t. This should obviously depend on the effort he has put up in the past, so we can write this probability as

$$P_k(e_1, \ldots, e_t)$$

Clearly the P_k functions are unobservable. However, they will allow us to derive observable transition probabilities. To see this, consider the problem that the executive faces. He must choose his effort levels e_t so as to maximize his utility, given the incentive schedule summed up in the functions P_k. The solution of this program can be written as

$$e_t = E_t(K_1, \ldots, K_t)$$

where K_t is the job level of the executive in period t. But by substituting into the P_k functions, we get the promotion probability of an executive at period t given the history of his past promotions:

$$\Pi_t(K_1, ..., K_t) = P_{K_t}(E_1(K_1), ..., E_t(K_1, ..., K_t))$$

Now these promotion probabilities can be observed from the data, so we can use them to test alternative theories. For instance, an adverse selection model with job-specific abilities would imply that Π_t only depends on K_t and on the level seniority, that is, the time spent in job level K_t. An adverse selection model with full commitment would imply that the promotion process is memoryless: Π_t only depends on K_t. So would some moral hazard models (in particular, if preferences are CARA). Bourguignon-Chiappori (1990) test these properties and reject them all. They thus conclude that the incentive system used in the firm is richer than what these simple theories would imply.

My second example is taken from Chiappori-Salanié-Valentin (1997). They show that several models of the labor market (most notably the learning model of Harris-Holmstrom 1982) have the property that $\Pi_t(K_1, ..., K_t)$ should be a decreasing function of $(K_1, ..., K_{t-1})$. In their terminology, this implies that "early starters" (who got promoted early) have a lower promotion probability than "late beginners" (who were promoted late but eventually caught up with the early starters). They find that their data supports this conclusion.

8.2.2 Exploiting Insurance Data

One peculiar feature of, say, car insurance is that performances (i.e., accidents) are usually recorded by insurance companies. Thus having access to data from an insurance company that sells car insurance should provide us with excellent opportunities for testing moral hazard models. Without going into details, let me give two examples. The first one is a reduced-form test for the presence of asymmetric information. Assume that we can establish that drivers who choose comprehensive insurance have a higher probability of accident; then this would strongly point to the presence of adverse selection (where riskier drivers choose better coverage) or of moral hazard (where drivers who are more completely covered make less self-protection efforts). Chiappori-Salanié (1997) pursue this strategy on French car insurance data; surprisingly, they find little evidence of asymmetric information on this particular market. My second example again concerns the choice of comprehensive versus minimum coverage. This provides us with much useful information, since drivers must trade off between the quality of their coverage and its cost, taking into account the fact that if they choose comprehensive insurance, they will be less cautious, have more accidents, and therefore (since most insurance companies practice experience rating) pay a higher premium in the future. Thus the structural model we must estimate has strong dynamic features.

8.3 Conclusion

It is perhaps early to provide a temptative conclusion. I have focused in this chapter on structural models because that is where the more interesting developments have taken place recently, in my judgment. There have been many interesting reduced-form studies, however. This includes, for instance, the work of Joskow (1987, 1990) on coal markets, which shows, inter alia, that contracts tend to be more durable and less frequently renegotiated when relationship-specific investments predominate.

There is a common perception that it is very difficult to get data on contracts. Recent papers seem to prove that it is not quite true. For instance, data on auctions are widely available, and there is still much interesting work to be done in that area, such as to move from the independent private values model to the more general affiliated values model of Milgrom-Weber (1982). Insurance companies also have a wealth of data and seem more and more willing to open it to economists. Firm-level personnel data also are a very rich source that should allow us to test labor economics models adapted from the theory of contracts, as shown by Baker-Gibbs-Holmstrom (1994a, b).

References

Baker, G., M. Gibbs, and B. Holmstrom. 1994a. The internal economics of the firm: Evidence from personnel data. *Quarterly Journal of Economics* 109:881–919.

Baker, G., M. Gibbs, and B. Holmstrom. 1994b. The wage policy of a firm. *Quarterly Journal of Economics* 109:921–55.

Bourguignon, F., and P. A. Chiappori. 1990. Executives' promotion in an internal labor market: An econometric analysis. *Essays in Honor of Edmond Malinvaud* vol. 3. Cambridge: MIT Press, pp. 25–49.

Chiappori, P.-A., and B. Salanié. 1997. Empirical Contract Theory: The Case of Insurance Data. *European Economic Review* 41:943–950.

Chiappori, P.-A., B. Salanié, and J. Valentin. 1996. Early starters vs. late beginners. CREST DP9623.

Elyakime, B., J.-J. Laffont, P. Loisel, and Q. Vuong. 1994. First-price sealed-bid auctions with secret reservation prices. *Annales d'Economie et de Statistique* 34:115–41.

Harris, M., and B. Holmstrom. 1982. A theory of wage dynamics. *Review of Economic Studies* 49:315–34.

Hendricks, K., and H. Paarsch. 1995. A survey of recent empirical work concerning auctions. *Canadian Journal of Economics* 28:403–26.

Joskow, P. 1987. Contract duration and relationship-specific investments. *American Economic Review* 77:168–85.

Joskow, P. 1990. The performance of long-term contracts: Further evidence from coal markets. *Rand Journal of Economics* 21:251–74.

Laffont, J.-J. 1995. Game theory and empirical economics: The case of auction data. IDEI-Toulouse DP55.

Laffont, J.-J., and M. S. Matoussi. 1995. Moral hazard, financial constraints and sharecropping in El Oulja. *Review of Economic Studies* 62:381–99.

Laffont, J.-J., H. Ossard, and Q. Vuong. 1995. Econometrics of first-price auctions. *Econometrica* 63:953–80.

Laroque, G., and B. Salanié. 1989. Estimation of multimarket fix-price models: An application of pseudo-maximum likelihood methods. *Econometrica* 57:831–60.

Milgrom, P., and R. Weber. 1982. A theory of auctions and competitive bidding. *Econometrica* 50:1089–1122.

Murphy, K. 1986. Incentives, learning, and compensation: A theoretical and empirical investigation of managerial labor contracts. *Rand Journal of Economics* 17:59–76.

Paarsch, H. 1992. Deciding between the common and private value paradigms in empirical models of auctions. *Journal of Econometrics* 51:192–215.

Slade, M. 1996. Multitask agency and contract choice: An empirical exploration. *International Economic Review* 37:465–86.

Vuong, Q. 1989. Likelihood ratio tests for model selection and non-nested hypotheses. *Econometrica* 57:307–34.

Wolak, F. 1994. An econometric analysis of the asymmetric information, regulator-utility interaction. *Annales d'Economie et de Statistique* 34:13–69.

Appendix

Some Noncooperative Game Theory

In solving a problem of this sort, the grand thing is to be able to reason backwards.
Arthur Conan Doyle, *A Study in Scarlet.*

This appendix has limited ambitions: It only aims at presenting some equilibrium concepts for noncooperative games that are used in this book (especially in chapters 4 and 6). Readers interested in a more detailed study of these concepts can turn to chapter 11 of Tirole (1988), to chapter 12 of Kreps (1990a), or to the book by Fudenberg-Tirole (1991). This appendix presumes that the readers already know what a game is and how it is modeled.

I will consider an n-player game. Player i has strategies $s_i \in S_i$ and a utility function denoted by $u_i(s_1, \ldots, s_n)$. I will denote mixed strategies by σ_i. If $\sigma = (\sigma_1, \ldots, \sigma_n)$ is a vector of strategies, σ_{-i} represents the vector $(\sigma_1, \ldots, \sigma_{i-1}, \sigma_{i+1}, \ldots, \sigma_n)$. Recall that a mixed strategy σ_i is called *totally mixed* if it has full support on the set of pure strategies S_i. By a slight abuse of notation, I will denote $u_i(\sigma)$ the expected utility of player i when players adopt mixed strategies $\sigma = (\sigma_1, \ldots, \sigma_n)$. Assume, for instance, that the strategy spaces are finite, and let $\sigma_i(s_i)$ be the weight of pure strategy s_i in the mixed strategy σ_i; we then have

$$
u_i(\sigma) = \sum_{s_1 \in S_1} \ldots \sum_{s_n \in S_n} \left(\prod_{j=1}^{n} \sigma_j(s_j) \right) u_i(s)
$$

A.1   Games of Perfect Information

A.1.1   Nash Equilibrium

A Nash equilibrium is a strategy profile $(\sigma_1^*, \ldots, \sigma_n^*)$ such that each σ_i^* is a best response to the equilibrium strategies σ_{-i}^* of the other players:

$$\forall i, \quad \sigma_i^* \in \arg\max_{\sigma_i} u_i(\sigma_i, \sigma_{-i}^*)$$

A.1.2   Subgame-Perfect Equilibrium

Dynamic games are usually described through their extensive form, which represents the sequential unrolling of the game through a *game tree*, as in figure A.1 in which player 1 chooses between strategies T and B and player 2 then chooses between strategies t and b; the utilities achieved by both players are indicated on the right of the terminal nodes of the tree.

The extensive form makes it easy to define subgames that correspond to various branches of the game tree. Thus there are three subgames in the previous example: the game itself, and the two subgames starting with the nodes marked by a 2. Each strategy conceived for the whole game engenders strategies in each subgame. When global strategies form a Nash equilibrium, the strategies induced in each subgame must form a Nash equilibrium in each subgame that is effec-

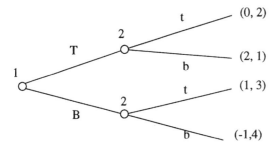

Figure A.1
An extensive-form game

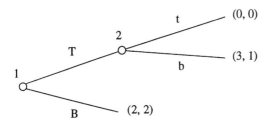

Figure A.2
Subgame-perfect equilibria

tively reached at equilibrium. On the other hand, Nash equilibrium may prescribe strategies that are not a Nash equilibrium in a subgame that is not reached in equilibrium. Some Nash equilibria may thus rest on the fact that player 1 threatens player 2 with a punishment if player 2 deviates from equilibrium, even though this punishment may hurt player 1 himself. If player 2 were in fact to deviate from equilibrium, then it would not be in player 1's interest to carry out his threat: This type of threat therefore is not credible.

The concept of subgame-perfect equilibrium was designed to eliminate such noncredible threats. It is defined as a strategy profile that is a Nash equilibrium in all subgames, *including those that are not reached in equilibrium.*

Consider, for instance, the game depicted in figure A.2. There are two Nash equilibria in this game: In the first equilibrium, denoted by (T, b), player 1 plays T and player 2 plays b; in the second equilibrium, denoted by B, player 1 plays B and the game stops. However, B is a Nash equilibrium only because player 1 anticipates that 2 will play t if 1 plays T; since t is a dominated strategy for 2, this cannot be a subgame-perfect equilibrium. (T, b) in fact is the only subgame-perfect equilibrium of this game.

In finite-horizon games the search for subgame-perfect equilibria uses Kuhn's algorithm of backward induction:[1] We first look for Nash equilibria on the terminal branches of the game, then we affect

---

1. This mode of thinking was also favored by Sherlock Holmes, as shown by the quotation that opens this chapter.

to the nodes the "reduced utilities" thus computed, and we iterate the algorithm until the whole game is solved. In the above example this procedure affects to player 1's T strategy the utility vector $(3, 1)$, since b is player 2's preferred strategy. Player 1 then chooses T, which gives him a higher utility than B.

A.2   Games of Incomplete Information

Some authors make a subtle distinction between games of incomplete information and games of imperfect information. In games of imperfect information, the player is not perfectly informed of what other players have done before him; in games of incomplete information, players do not know all characteristics (or types) of their opponents.

In fact every game of incomplete information can be transformed into a game of imperfect information by adding a $(n + 1)$th player, Nature, which randomly picks the types of the other n players before the game itself starts. This distinction therefore is not very relevant. In any case I will only need to study here games of incomplete information.

A.2.1   Bayesian Equilibrium

Each player i now has a type θ_i which I will take in a finite set to simplify exposition; his utility is $u_i(s_1, \ldots, s_n, \theta_i)$, and the strategy he chooses may of course depend on his type.

Types are drawn from a joint distribution $\pi(\theta_1, \ldots, \theta_n)$. I will assume that the prior beliefs of the players are consistent with this joint distribution:[2] The prior of player i is the conditional distribution $\pi_i(\theta_{-i} \mid \theta_i)$, where $\theta_{-i} = (\theta_1, \ldots, \theta_{i-1}, \theta_{i+1}, \ldots, \theta_n)$.

The analogous concept to the Nash equilibrium in this setup is the Bayesian equilibrium. A type-dependent strategy profile

---

2. This *common priors* assumption is almost universal in the literature.

$$\left(\sigma_1^*(\theta_1), \ldots, \sigma_n^*(\theta_n)\right)$$

is a Bayesian equilibrium if every player chooses his "expected best response":

$$\forall \theta, \forall i, \sigma_i^*(\theta_i) \in \arg\max_{\sigma_i} \sum_{\theta_{-i}} \pi_i(\theta_{-i} \mid \theta_i) \, u_i(\sigma_i, \sigma_{-i}^*(\theta_{-i}), \theta_i)$$

We could also define a subgame-perfect Bayesian equilibrium concept by imposing that strategies form a Bayesian equilibrium in each subgame. This notion is only used in practice as a building block for perfect Bayesian equilibrium or its refinements, to which we now turn.

A.2.2 Perfect Bayesian Equilibrium

Bayesian equilibrium does not take into account the fact that players may learn their opponents' types by observing their play, since each move by a player may reveal information on his type. Assume, for instance, that the first player, who has two possible types, may play L or R. Assume also that the first type of player 1 has a higher utility in branch L, while its second type has a higher utility in branch R. Then the first type will tend to choose L and the second type will tend to choose R. When the second player observes that the first player chose to play L, he logically should revise his prior belief on player 1 and increase his prior that player 1 is of the first type. The concept of perfect Bayesian equilibrium aims at formalizing this process of updating beliefs, by modeling the mutual links between equilibrium strategies and beliefs.

At each node of the game, the player whose turn it is to play has an information set that describes his uncertainty as to what types the other players are, and beliefs π that are a probability distribution on this information set; accordingly these beliefs evolve as the game unfolds. These beliefs thus specify, at each node of the game, a probability distribution on the types of each other player.

Perfect Bayesian equilibria integrate two requirements:

• *Sequential rationality.* The strategies σ played at equilibrium must form a subgame-perfect Bayesian equilibrium, given the beliefs π at every node.

• *Bayesian consistency.* The beliefs π at every node must obtain through Bayesian updating of prior beliefs, given the equilibrium strategies σ.

"Bayesian updating" means that players use Bayes's rule whenever it is possible. Assume, for instance, that player 1 has only two possible types θ_1 and θ_2 that are a priori equiprobable and two possible strategies T and B. Let p_i be the probability that type θ_i of player 1 plays T in equilibrium. Then the probability that player 1 plays T in equilibrium is

$$\frac{p_1 + p_2}{2}$$

If $p_1 + p_2 \neq 0$, Bayes's rule allows us to compute the beliefs of player 2 after player 1 has played T: Player 2 then assigns probability $p_1/(p_1 + p_2)$ to type θ_1. On the other hand, if $p_1 = p_2 = 0$, that is, if T is never played in equilibrium, then Bayes's rule does not apply and player 2's beliefs are unrestricted after T.

A perfect Bayesian equilibrium thus is a n-tuple of strategies σ and a n-tuple of beliefs π at every node such that

• the strategies σ form a subgame-perfect Bayesian equilibrium, given the beliefs π,

• the beliefs π are obtained from the prior beliefs by applying Bayes' rule at every node that is reached with nonzero probability in equilibrium when players follow the strategies σ.

Figure A.3 sums up the mutual determination of beliefs and strategies in a perfect Bayesian equilibrium.

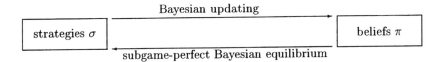

Figure A.3
The perfect Bayesian equilibrium

A.2.3 Refinements of Perfect Bayesian Equilibrium

Perfect Bayesian equilibrium does not restrict out-of-equilibrium beliefs at all: If a node of the game is never reached in equilibrium, then Bayes' rule has no bite there. In many games it will therefore be possible to support a large number and sometimes a continuum of perfect Bayesian equilibria by choosing particular out-of-equilibrium beliefs.[3]

Several more restrictive equilibrium concepts have been proposed to remedy this. They all aim at limiting possible beliefs when an out-of-equilibrium move takes place. I will only present two of these refinements; they are the only ones used in this book.

Sequential Equilibrium
Sequential equilibrium reinforces the Bayesian consistency requirement by imposing that out-of-equilibrium beliefs be the limit of beliefs that are generated by totally mixed strategies that are close to equilibrium strategies. This definition exploits the fact that Bayes's rule uniquely determines beliefs when strategies are totally mixed, since every node of the game then is reached with nonzero probability.

More formally, (σ, π) is a sequential equilibrium if the strategies σ are a subgame-perfect equilibrium given the beliefs π and if there exists a sequence of totally mixed strategies σ^n and a sequence of beliefs π^n such that

---

3. Chapter 4 presents a striking example.

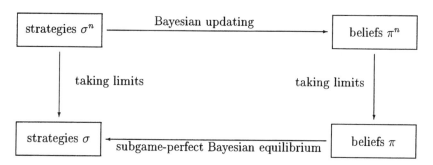

Figure A.4
The sequential equilibrium

- π^n is obtained from σ^n by applying Bayes's rule in every node of the game,

- $\lim_{n\to\infty}(\sigma^n, \pi^n) = (\sigma, \pi.)$

Note that we *do not* require that the strategies σ^n form a subgame-perfect Bayesian equilibrium given the corresponding beliefs π^n, only that this is true at the limit. Figure A.4 shows how a sequential equilibrium is computed.

Selten also proposed a concept of trembling-hand perfect equilibrium that relies on a robustness property when equilibrium strategies are slightly perturbed.[4] Kreps-Wilson (1982) showed that the set of trembling-hand perfect equilibria coincides with that of sequential equilibria in almost all finite games.

Intuitive Equilibrium

Signaling models are a typical example in which the game has a very large number of perfect Bayesian equilibria; chapter 4 shows that sequential equilibrium does not solve this difficulty. To solve these games, Cho-Kreps (1987) proposed what they call the "intuitive criterion." This imposes that we give zero probability to the type θ of any player who has just played an out-of-equilibrium strategy s

---

4. The underlying idea is that the equilibrium should not change too much when players are allowed to make mistakes with a small probability.

when that strategy is dominated for type θ. By "dominated," we mean here that whatever beliefs the other players adopt after observing s, their best responses can only give type θ a lower utility than what he gets in equilibrium. An intuitive equilibrium then is a perfect Bayesian equilibrium that passes the intuitive criterion.

Giving a precise definition of the intuitive criterion involves a lot of notation, so I will only give here a rough outline. Start from a perfect Bayesian equilibrium. Assume that at some stage in the game, type θ's equilibrium strategy is some s_0 and that the other players' equilibrium response is s_0' so that in the end θ's expected payoff is $U(s_0, s_0', \theta)$. Now let s be a possible deviation by θ. If the other players revise their beliefs to μ when they observe s, they will then play their best response $s'(\mu, s)$, and θ will eventually obtain $U(s, s'(\mu, s), \theta)$. The intuitive criterion rejects perfect Bayesian equilibria which are supported by out-of-equilibrium beliefs such that

$$\max_{\mu} U(s, s'(\mu, s), \theta) < U(s_0, s_0', \theta)$$

and yet μ gives some weight to type θ.[5]

This equilibrium concept thus formalizes the idea according to which some deviations from equilibrium strategies can only be reasonable for some types: Type θ will only deviate if he has some hope that the other players may react in ways that increase his utility. Any other deviation by θ would be counterproductive, and the intuitive criterion therefore excludes it. As chapter 4 shows, the intuitive criterion is successful at selecting an equilibrium in signaling games, at least with only two types.[6] The trouble with the intuitive criterion is that as all *forward induction* arguments,[7] it relies on counterfactual

---

5. There is a slight technicality here: It might be that the inequality in the text holds for all types θ, in which case μ would have total weight zero. Then the intuitive criterion should not be applied.

6. With three types, one needs stronger refinements to select a unique equilibrium.

7. The idea of forward induction is that if your opponent deviates from equilibrium behavior, you should not presume that this is due to an unintended error (as in trembling-hand heuristics); you should instead keep assuming that he is fully rational and draw whatever conclusions you may from his deviation.

"speeches" by deviating players that should (ideally!) be modeled in a communication game.

The quest for the ultimate refinement of perfect Bayesian equilibrium was buoyant at the beginning of the 1980s[8] but is much less active now. The consensus view seems to be that game theorists should devote more attention to issues of robustness and learning that do not presume that players are hyperrational (Kreps 1990b gives convincing reasons to turn to such an approach).

References

Cho, I. K., and D. Kreps. 1987. Signaling games and stable equilibria. *Quarterly Journal of Economics* 102:179–221.

Fudenberg, D., and J. Tirole. 1991. *Game Theory*. Cambridge: MIT Press.

Kreps, D. 1990a. *A Course in Microeconomic Theory*. Princeton: Princeton University Press.

Kreps, D. 1990b. *Game Theory and Economic Modeling*. Oxford: Oxford University Press.

Kreps, D., and R. Wilson. 1982. Sequential equilibria. *Econometrica* 50:863–94.

Tirole, J. 1988. *Industrial Organization*. Cambridge: MIT Press.

Van Damme, E. 1991. *Stability and Perfection of Nash Equilibria*. New York: Springer-Verlag.

---

8. Van Damme (1991) gives a very thorough survey of this literature.

Index